Cram101 Textbook Outlines to accompany:

Child Development

Laura E. Berk, 8th Edition

A Cram101 Inc. publication (c) 2010.

PRACTICE EXAMS.

Get all of the self-teaching practice exams for each chapter of this textbook at **www.Cram101.com** and ace the tests. Here is an example:

Chapter 1

Child Development
Laura E. Berk, 8th Edition,
All Material Written and Prepared by Cram101

I WANT A BETTER GRADE.   Items 1 - 50 of 100. ▶

1 _____ is a transitional stage of physical and mental human development that occurs between childhood and adulthood. This transition involves biological (i.e. pubertal), social, and psychological changes, though the biological or physiological ones are the easiest to measure objectively. Historically, puberty has been heavily associated with teenagers and the onset of adolescent development.

  ⭕ Adolescence   ⭕ Aaron Loves Angela

  ⭕ Abandoned child syndrome   ⭕ Abigail Garner

2 In _____ theory psychology, _____ is a product of the activity of a number of behavioral systems that have proximity to a person, e.g. a mother, as a predictable outcome. The concept of there being an "_____" behavior, stage, and process, to which a growing person remains in proximity to another was developed beginning in 1956 by British developmental psychologist John Bowlby. According to Bowlby, the concept of proximity _____ has its origins in Charles Darwin"s 1856 Origin of Species, which "sees instinctive behavior as the outcome of behavioral structures that are activated by certain conditions and terminated by other conditions", Sigmund Freud"s 1905 Three Essays on the Theory of Sexuality and his 1915 Instincts and their Vicissitudes, which according to Bowlby "postulates part-instincts, differentiates the aim of an instinct, namely the conditions that terminate instinctive behavior, and its function, and notes how labile are the objects towards which any particular sort of instinctive behavior is directed", and Konrad Lorenz"s 1937 theory of imprinting.

  ⭕ Attachment   ⭕ Aaron Loves Angela

  ⭕ Abandoned child syndrome   ⭕ Abigail Garner

3 An _____ or baby is the term used to refer to the very young offspring of humans and other primates.

With Cram101.com online, you also have access to extensive reference material.

You will nail those essays and papers. Here is an example from a Cram101 Biology text:

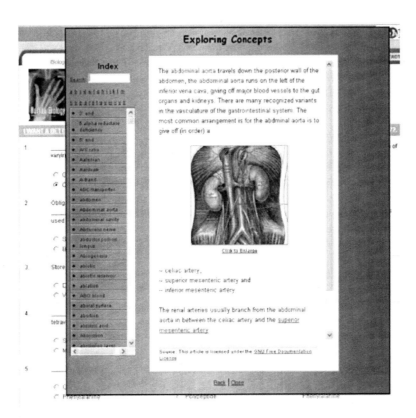

Visit **www.Cram101.com**, click Sign Up at the top of the screen, and enter DK73DW7611 in the promo code box on the registration screen. Access to www.Cram101.com is normally $9.95 per month, but because you have purchased this book, your access fee is only $4.95 per month, cancel at any time. Sign up and stop highlighting textbooks forever.

Learning System

Cram101 Textbook Outlines is a learning system. The notes in this book are the highlights of your textbook, you will never have to highlight a book again.

How to use this book. Take this book to class, it is your notebook for the lecture. The notes and highlights on the left hand side of the pages follow the outline and order of the textbook. All you have to do is follow along while your instructor presents the lecture. Circle the items emphasized in class and add other important information on the right side. With Cram101 Textbook Outlines you'll spend less time writing and more time listening. Learning becomes more efficient.

Cram101.com Online

Increase your studying efficiency by using Cram101.com's practice tests and online reference material. It is the perfect complement to Cram101 Textbook Outlines. Use self-teaching matching tests or simulate in-class testing with comprehensive multiple choice tests, or simply use Cram's true and false tests for quick review. Cram101.com even allows you to enter your in-class notes for an integrated studying format combining the textbook notes with your class notes.

Visit **www.Cram101.com**, click Sign Up at the top of the screen, and enter **DK73DW7611** in the promo code box on the registration screen. Access to www.Cram101.com is normally $9.95 per month, but because you have purchased this book, your access fee is only $4.95 per month. Sign up and stop highlighting textbooks forever.

Child Development
Laura E. Berk, 8th

CONTENTS

Adolescence	Adolescence is a transitional stage of physical and mental human development that occurs between childhood and adulthood. This transition involves biological (i.e. pubertal), social, and psychological changes, though the biological or physiological ones are the easiest to measure objectively. Historically, puberty has been heavily associated with teenagers and the onset of adolescent development.
Attachment	In Attachment theory psychology, Attachment is a product of the activity of a number of behavioral systems that have proximity to a person, e.g. a mother, as a predictable outcome. The concept of there being an "Attachment" behavior, stage, and process, to which a growing person remains in proximity to another was developed beginning in 1956 by British developmental psychologist John Bowlby. According to Bowlby, the concept of proximity Attachment has its origins in Charles Darwin"s 1856 Origin of Species, which "sees instinctive behavior as the outcome of behavioral structures that are activated by certain conditions and terminated by other conditions", Sigmund Freud"s 1905 Three Essays on the Theory of Sexuality and his 1915 Instincts and their Vicissitudes, which according to Bowlby "postulates part-instincts, differentiates the aim of an instinct, namely the conditions that terminate instinctive behavior, and its function, and notes how labile are the objects towards which any particular sort of instinctive behavior is directed", and Konrad Lorenz"s 1937 theory of imprinting.
Infant	An Infant or baby is the term used to refer to the very young offspring of humans and other primates. The term Infant derives from the Latin word infans, meaning "unable to speak." It is typically applied to children between the ages of 1 month and 12 months . However, definitions vary between birth and 3 years of age.
Child	A Child (plural: Child ren) is a human being between the stages of birth and puberty. The legal definition of Child generally refers to a minor, otherwise known as a person younger than the age of majority. Child may also describe a relationship with a parent or authority figure, or signify group membership in a clan, tribe, or religion; it can also signify being strongly affected by a specific time, place, or circumstance, as in "a Child of nature" or "a Child of the Sixties." The United Nations Convention on the Rights of the Child defines a Child as "every human being below the age of 18 years unless under the law applicable to the Child majority is attained earlier." Biologically, a Child is anyone in the developmental stage of Child hood, between infancy and adulthood.
Child development	Child development refers to the biological and psychological changes that occur in human beings between birth and the end of adolescence, as the individual progresses from dependency to increasing autonomy. Because these developmental changes may be strongly influenced by genetic factors and events during prenatal life, genetics and prenatal development are usually included as part of the study of Child development. Related terms include "developmental psychology", referring to development throughout the lifespan and "pediatrics", the branch of medicine relating to the care of children.
Emerging adulthood	Emerging adulthood is a phase of the life span between adolescence and full-fledged adulthood, proposed by Jeffrey Arnett in a 2000 article in the American Psychologist (summary of article 469.)

Head Start	Head Start is a program of the United States Department of Health and Human Services that provides comprehensive education, health, nutrition, and parent involvement services to low-income children and their families. Head Start began in 1964 and was later updated by the Head Start Act of 1981. It is the longest-running program to address systemic poverty in the United States.
Childbirth	Childbirth is the culmination of a human pregnancy or gestation period with birth of one or more newborn infants from a woman"s uterus. The process of normal human Childbirth is categorized in three stages of labour: the shortening and dilation of the cervix, descent and birth of the infant, and birth of the placenta.. In some cases, Childbirth is achieved through caesarean section, the removal of the neonate through a surgical incision in the abdomen, rather than through vaginal birth.
Childhood	Childhood is a broad term usually applied to the phase of development in humans between infancy and adulthood. In many countries there is an age of majority when Childhood ends and a person legally becomes an adult. The age can range anywhere from 13 to 21, with 18 being the most common.
Intelligence	Intelligence is an umbrella term used to describe a property of the mind that encompasses many related abilities, such as the capacities to reason, to plan, to solve problems, to think abstractly, to comprehend ideas, to use language, and to learn. There are several ways to define Intelligence. In some cases, Intelligence may include traits such as creativity, personality, character, knowledge, or wisdom.
Parent	A Parent is a mother or father; one who sires or gives birth to and/or nurtures and raises an offspring. The different roles of Parent s vary throughout the tree of life, and are especially complex in human culture. Like mothers, fathers may be categorised according to their biological, social or legal relationship with the child.
Play	Play is a rite and a quality of mind in engaging with one"s worldview. Play refers to a range of voluntary, intrinsically motivated activities that are normally associated with pleasure and enjoyment. Play may consist of amusing, pretend or imaginary interpersonal and intrapersonal interactions or interplay.
Parenting	Parenting is the process of promoting and supporting the physical, emotional, social, and intellectual development of a child from infancy to adulthood. Parenting refers to the activity of raising a child rather than the biological relationship. In the case of humans, it is usually done by the biological parents of the child in question, although governments and society take a role as well.

Youth	Youth is the period between childhood and adulthood, described as the period of physical and psychological development from the onset of puberty to maturity and early adulthood. Definitions of the specific age range that constitutes Youth vary. An individual"s actual maturity may not correspond to their chronological age, as immature individuals exist at all ages.
Breastfeeding	Breastfeeding is the feeding of an infant or young child with breast milk directly from human breasts rather than from a baby bottle or other container. Babies have a sucking reflex that enables them to suck and swallow milk. Most mothers can breastfeed for six months or more, without the addition of infant formula or solid food.
Autism	Autism is a brain development disorder characterized by impaired social interaction and communication, and by restricted and repetitive behavior. These signs all begin before a child is three years old. Autism affects many parts of the brain; how this occurs is not understood.
Learning	Learning is acquiring new knowledge, behaviors, skills, values, preferences or understanding, and may involve synthesizing different types of information. The ability to learn is possessed by humans, animals and some machines. Progress over time tends to follow Learning curves.
Evolutionary developmental psychology	Evolutionary developmental psychology, (or Evolutionary developmental psychology), is the application of the basic principles of Darwinian evolution, particularly natural selection, to explain contemporary human development. It involves the study of the genetic and environmental mechanisms that underlie the universal development of social and cognitive competencies and the evolved epigenetic (gene-environment interactions) processes that adapt these competencies to local conditions; it assumes that not only are behaviors and cognitions that characterize adults the product of natural selection pressures operating over the course of evolution, but so also are characteristics of children"s behaviors and minds. It further proposes that an evolutionary account would provide some insight into not only predictable stages of ontogeny, but into specific differences between individuals as well.
Imprinting	Imprinting is the term used in psychology and ethology to describe any kind of phase-sensitive learning (learning occurring at a particular age or a particular life stage) that is rapid and apparently independent of the consequences of behavior. It was first used to describe situations in which an animal or person learns the characteristics of some stimulus, which is therefore said to be "imprinted" onto the subject. The best known form of Imprinting is filial Imprinting, in which a young animal learns the characteristics of its parent.
Sibling	A Sibling is a brother or a sister; that is, any person who shares at least one of the same parents. In most societies throughout the world, Sibling s usually grow up together and spend a good deal of their childhood with each other. This genetic and physical closeness may be marked by the development of strong emotional associations such as love or enmity.
Theory of cognitive development	The Theory of cognitive development, first developed by Jean Piaget, proposes that there are four distinct, increasingly sophisticated stages of mental representation that children pass through on their way to an adult level of intelligence.

The four stages, roughly correlated with age, are as follows:

- Sensorimotor period (years 0 to 2)
- Preoperational period (years 2 to 7)
- Concrete operational period (years 7 to 12)
- Formal operational period (years 12 and up)

The Sensorimotor Stage is the first of the four stages of cognitive development. "In this stage, infants construct an understanding of the world by coordinating sensory experiences with physical, motoric actions." "Infants gain knowledge of the world from the physical actions they perform on it." "An infant progresses from reflexive, instinctual action at birth to the beginning of symbolic thought toward the end of the stage." "Piaget divided the sensorimotor stage into six sub-stages":

"By the end of the sensorimotor period, objects are both separate from the self and permanent." "Object permanence is the understanding that objects continue to exist even when they cannot be seen, heard, or touched." "Acquiring the sense of object permanence is one of the infant"s most important accomplishments, according to Piaget."

The Preoperational stage is the second of four stages of cognitive development. By observing sequences of play, Piaget was able to demonstrate that towards the end of the second year, a qualitatively new kind of psychological functioning occurs.

Ecological systems theory

Ecological Systems Theory specifies four types of nested environmental systems, with bi-directional influences within and between the systems.

The theory was developed by Urie Bronfenbrenner, generally regarded as one of the world"s leading scholars in the field of developmental psychology.

The four systems:

- Microsystem: Immediate environments
- Mesosystem: A system comprising connections between immediate environments
- Exosystem: External environmental settings which only indirectly affect development
- Macrosystem: The larger cultural context

Later, a fifth system was added:

- Chronosystem: The patterning of environmental events and transitions over the course of life.

The person"s own biology may be considered part of the microsystem; thus the theory has recently sometimes been called "Bio-Ecological Systems Theory."

Per this theoretical construction, each system contains roles, norms and rules which may shape psychological development.

Sign language	Specialized sign language is sometimes used to communicate with infants and toddlers. While infants and toddlers have a desire to communicate their needs and wishes, they lack the ability to do so clearly because the production of speech lags behind cognitive ability in the first months and years of life. Proponents of baby sign language say that this gap between desire to communicate and ability often leads to frustration and tantrums.
Parental leave	Parental leave is an employee benefit that provides paid or unpaid time off work to care for a child or make arrangements for the child"s welfare. Often, the term Parental leave includes maternity, paternity, and adoption leave. In most western countries Parental leave is available for those who have worked for their current employer for a certain period of time.
Sibling relationships	Judy Dunn (a leading expert on sibling relationship) in 2007 described three important characteristics of Sibling relationships. Emotional quality of the relatioship: Both intensive postiive and negative emotions are often expressed by siblings toward each other. Many children and adolescents have mixed feelings toward their siblings.
Pregnancy	Pregnancy is the carrying of one or more offspring inside the uterus of a female. In a Pregnancy, there can be multiple gestations, as in the case of twins or triplets. Human Pregnancy is the most studied of all mammalian pregnancies.
Teenage pregnancy	Teenage pregnancy is defined as a teenaged or underage girl (usually within the ages of 13-19) becoming pregnant. The term in everyday speech usually refers to women who have not reached legal adulthood, which varies across the world, who become pregnant. The average age of menarche (first menstrual period) in the United States is 12 years old, though this figure varies by ethnicity and weight, and first ovulation occurs only irregularly until after this.
Mental retardation	Mental retardation is a generalized disorder, characterized by subaverage cognitive functioning and deficits in two or more adaptive behaviors with onset before the age of 18. Once focused almost entirely on cognition, the definition now includes both a component relating to mental functioning and one relating to individuals" functional skills in their environment. The term "Mental retardation" is a diagnostic term designed to capture and standardize a group of disconnected categories of mental functioning such as "idiot", "imbecile", and "moron" derived from early IQ tests, which acquired pejorative connotations in popular discourse over time.

Child	A Child (plural: Child ren) is a human being between the stages of birth and puberty. The legal definition of Child generally refers to a minor, otherwise known as a person younger than the age of majority. Child may also describe a relationship with a parent or authority figure, or signify group membership in a clan, tribe, or religion; it can also signify being strongly affected by a specific time, place, or circumstance, as in "a Child of nature" or "a Child of the Sixties." The United Nations Convention on the Rights of the Child defines a Child as "every human being below the age of 18 years unless under the law applicable to the Child majority is attained earlier." Biologically, a Child is anyone in the developmental stage of Child hood, between infancy and adulthood.
Child development	Child development refers to the biological and psychological changes that occur in human beings between birth and the end of adolescence, as the individual progresses from dependency to increasing autonomy. Because these developmental changes may be strongly influenced by genetic factors and events during prenatal life, genetics and prenatal development are usually included as part of the study of Child development. Related terms include "developmental psychology", referring to development throughout the lifespan and "pediatrics", the branch of medicine relating to the care of children.
Intelligence	Intelligence is an umbrella term used to describe a property of the mind that encompasses many related abilities, such as the capacities to reason, to plan, to solve problems, to think abstractly, to comprehend ideas, to use language, and to learn. There are several ways to define Intelligence. In some cases, Intelligence may include traits such as creativity, personality, character, knowledge, or wisdom.
Play	Play is a rite and a quality of mind in engaging with one"s worldview. Play refers to a range of voluntary, intrinsically motivated activities that are normally associated with pleasure and enjoyment. Play may consist of amusing, pretend or imaginary interpersonal and intrapersonal interactions or interplay.
Parent	A Parent is a mother or father; one who sires or gives birth to and/or nurtures and raises an offspring. The different roles of Parent s vary throughout the tree of life, and are especially complex in human culture. Like mothers, fathers may be categorised according to their biological, social or legal relationship with the child.
Sibling	A Sibling is a brother or a sister; that is, any person who shares at least one of the same parents. In most societies throughout the world, Sibling s usually grow up together and spend a good deal of their childhood with each other. This genetic and physical closeness may be marked by the development of strong emotional associations such as love or enmity.
Sibling relationships	Judy Dunn (a leading expert on sibling relationship) in 2007 described three important characteristics of Sibling relationships. Emotional quality of the relatioship: Both intensive postiive and negative emotions are often expressed by siblings toward each other. Many children and adolescents have mixed feelings toward their siblings.

Adult	The term Adult has at least three distinct meanings. It can indicate a biologically grown or mature person. It may also mean a plant, animal, or person who has reached full growth or alternatively is capable of reproduction, or the classification legal Adult, generally determined as a person who has attained the legally fixed age of majority; as opposed to a minor.
Youth	Youth is the period between childhood and adulthood, described as the period of physical and psychological development from the onset of puberty to maturity and early adulthood. Definitions of the specific age range that constitutes Youth vary. An individual"s actual maturity may not correspond to their chronological age, as immature individuals exist at all ages.
Adolescence	Adolescence is a transitional stage of physical and mental human development that occurs between childhood and adulthood. This transition involves biological (i.e. pubertal), social, and psychological changes, though the biological or physiological ones are the easiest to measure objectively. Historically, puberty has been heavily associated with teenagers and the onset of adolescent development.
Society for Research in Child Development	The Society for Research in Child Development is a professional society for the field of developmental psychology, focusing specifically on child development. It is a multidisciplinary, not-for-profit, professional association with a membership of approximately 5,500 researchers, practitioners, and human development professionals from over 50 countries. The purposes of the society are to promote multidisciplinary research in the field of human development, to foster the exchange of information among scientists and other professionals of various disciplines, and to encourage applications of research findings.

Birth	Birth is the act or process of bearing or bringing forth offspring . The offspring is brought forth from the mother. Different forms of Birth are oviparity, vivipary or ovovivipary.
Play	Play is a rite and a quality of mind in engaging with one"s worldview. Play refers to a range of voluntary, intrinsically motivated activities that are normally associated with pleasure and enjoyment. Play may consist of amusing, pretend or imaginary interpersonal and intrapersonal interactions or interplay.
Pregnancy	Pregnancy is the carrying of one or more offspring inside the uterus of a female. In a Pregnancy, there can be multiple gestations, as in the case of twins or triplets. Human Pregnancy is the most studied of all mammalian pregnancies.
Adolescence	Adolescence is a transitional stage of physical and mental human development that occurs between childhood and adulthood. This transition involves biological (i.e. pubertal), social, and psychological changes, though the biological or physiological ones are the easiest to measure objectively. Historically, puberty has been heavily associated with teenagers and the onset of adolescent development.
Mental retardation	Mental retardation is a generalized disorder, characterized by subaverage cognitive functioning and deficits in two or more adaptive behaviors with onset before the age of 18. Once focused almost entirely on cognition, the definition now includes both a component relating to mental functioning and one relating to individuals" functional skills in their environment. The term "Mental retardation" is a diagnostic term designed to capture and standardize a group of disconnected categories of mental functioning such as "idiot", "imbecile", and "moron" derived from early IQ tests, which acquired pejorative connotations in popular discourse over time.
Breastfeeding	Breastfeeding is the feeding of an infant or young child with breast milk directly from human breasts rather than from a baby bottle or other container. Babies have a sucking reflex that enables them to suck and swallow milk. Most mothers can breastfeed for six months or more, without the addition of infant formula or solid food.
Imprinting	Imprinting is the term used in psychology and ethology to describe any kind of phase-sensitive learning (learning occurring at a particular age or a particular life stage) that is rapid and apparently independent of the consequences of behavior. It was first used to describe situations in which an animal or person learns the characteristics of some stimulus, which is therefore said to be "imprinted" onto the subject. The best known form of Imprinting is filial Imprinting, in which a young animal learns the characteristics of its parent.
Child	A Child (plural: Child ren) is a human being between the stages of birth and puberty. The legal definition of Child generally refers to a minor, otherwise known as a person younger than the age of majority. Child may also describe a relationship with a parent or authority figure, or signify group membership in a clan, tribe, or religion; it can also signify being strongly affected by a specific time, place, or circumstance, as in "a Child of nature" or "a Child of the Sixties."

The United Nations Convention on the Rights of the Child defines a Child as "every human being below the age of 18 years unless under the law applicable to the Child majority is attained earlier." Biologically, a Child is anyone in the developmental stage of Child hood, between infancy and adulthood.

| Infant | An Infant or baby is the term used to refer to the very young offspring of humans and other primates. The term Infant derives from the Latin word infans, meaning "unable to speak." It is typically applied to children between the ages of 1 month and 12 months . However, definitions vary between birth and 3 years of age. |

| Learning | Learning is acquiring new knowledge, behaviors, skills, values, preferences or understanding, and may involve synthesizing different types of information. The ability to learn is possessed by humans, animals and some machines. Progress over time tends to follow Learning curves. |

| Autism | Autism is a brain development disorder characterized by impaired social interaction and communication, and by restricted and repetitive behavior. These signs all begin before a child is three years old. Autism affects many parts of the brain; how this occurs is not understood. |

| Day care | Day care or child care is care of a child during the day by a person other than the child"s legal guardians, typically performed by someone outside the child"s immediate family. Day care is typically an ongoing service during specific periods, such as the parents" time at work. The service is known as child care in the United Kingdom and Australia and Day care in North America (although child care also has a broader meaning.) |

| Childbirth | Childbirth is the culmination of a human pregnancy or gestation period with birth of one or more newborn infants from a woman"s uterus. The process of normal human Childbirth is categorized in three stages of labour: the shortening and dilation of the cervix, descent and birth of the infant, and birth of the placenta.. In some cases, Childbirth is achieved through caesarean section, the removal of the neonate through a surgical incision in the abdomen, rather than through vaginal birth. |

| Intelligence | Intelligence is an umbrella term used to describe a property of the mind that encompasses many related abilities, such as the capacities to reason, to plan, to solve problems, to think abstractly, to comprehend ideas, to use language, and to learn. There are several ways to define Intelligence. In some cases, Intelligence may include traits such as creativity, personality, character, knowledge, or wisdom. |

| Head Start | Head Start is a program of the United States Department of Health and Human Services that provides comprehensive education, health, nutrition, and parent involvement services to low-income children and their families. Head Start began in 1964 and was later updated by the Head Start Act of 1981. It is the longest-running program to address systemic poverty in the United States. . |

Parenting	Parenting is the process of promoting and supporting the physical, emotional, social, and intellectual development of a child from infancy to adulthood. Parenting refers to the activity of raising a child rather than the biological relationship. In the case of humans, it is usually done by the biological parents of the child in question, although governments and society take a role as well.
Ecological systems theory	Ecological Systems Theory specifies four types of nested environmental systems, with bi-directional influences within and between the systems. The theory was developed by Urie Bronfenbrenner, generally regarded as one of the world"s leading scholars in the field of developmental psychology. The four systems: • Microsystem: Immediate environments • Mesosystem: A system comprising connections between immediate environments • Exosystem: External environmental settings which only indirectly affect development • Macrosystem: The larger cultural context Later, a fifth system was added: • Chronosystem: The patterning of environmental events and transitions over the course of life. The person"s own biology may be considered part of the microsystem; thus the theory has recently sometimes been called "Bio-Ecological Systems Theory." Per this theoretical construction, each system contains roles, norms and rules which may shape psychological development.
Sign language	Specialized sign language is sometimes used to communicate with infants and toddlers. While infants and toddlers have a desire to communicate their needs and wishes, they lack the ability to do so clearly because the production of speech lags behind cognitive ability in the first months and years of life. Proponents of baby sign language say that this gap between desire to communicate and ability often leads to frustration and tantrums.
Family therapy	Family therapy, also referred to as couple and Family therapy and family systems therapy, is a branch of psychotherapy that works with families and couples in intimate relationships to nurture change and development. It tends to view change in terms of the systems of interaction between family members. It emphasizes family relationships as an important factor in psychological health.
Neurodevelopmental disorder	A Neurodevelopmental disorder is an impairment of the growth and development of the brain or central nervous system. One narrower use of the term refers to a disorder of brain function which affects emotion, learning ability and memory and which unfolds as the individual grows. The term is sometimes erroneously used as an exclusive synonym for autism and autism spectrum disorders.

Child abuse	Child abuse is the physical and/or psychological/emotional mistreatment of children. In the United States, the Centers for Disease Control and Prevention (CDC) define child maltreatment as any act or series of acts or commission or omission by a parent or other caregiver that results in harm, potential for harm, or threat of harm to a child. Most Child abuse occurs in a child"s home, with a smaller amount occurring in the organizations, schools or communities the child interacts with.
Attention-deficit/hyperactivity disorder	Attention-deficit/hyperactivity disorder is a neurobehavioral developmental disorder. Attention-deficit/hyperactivity disorderHD is defined as a "persistent pattern of inattention or hyperactivity--impulsivity that is more frequently displayed and more severe than is typically observed in individuals at a comparable level of development." While symptoms may appear innocent and merely annoying nuisances to observers, "if left untreated, the persistent and pervasive effects of Attention-deficit/hyperactivity disorderHD symptoms can insidiously and severely interfere with one"s ability to get the most out of education, fulfill one"s potential in the workplace, establish and maintain interpersonal relationships, and maintain a generally positive sense of self."[p.2] It is the most commonly diagnosed behavioral disorder in children, affecting about 3 to 5% of children globally with symptoms starting before seven years of age. Attention-deficit/hyperactivity disorderHD is generally a chronic disorder with 30 to 50% of those individuals diagnosed in childhood continuing to have symptoms into adulthood.
Attachment	In Attachment theory psychology, Attachment is a product of the activity of a number of behavioral systems that have proximity to a person, e.g. a mother, as a predictable outcome. The concept of there being an "Attachment" behavior, stage, and process, to which a growing person remains in proximity to another was developed beginning in 1956 by British developmental psychologist John Bowlby. According to Bowlby, the concept of proximity Attachment has its origins in Charles Darwin"s 1856 Origin of Species, which "sees instinctive behavior as the outcome of behavioral structures that are activated by certain conditions and terminated by other conditions", Sigmund Freud"s 1905 Three Essays on the Theory of Sexuality and his 1915 Instincts and their Vicissitudes, which according to Bowlby "postulates part-instincts, differentiates the aim of an instinct, namely the conditions that terminate instinctive behavior, and its function, and notes how labile are the objects towards which any particular sort of instinctive behavior is directed", and Konrad Lorenz"s 1937 theory of imprinting.
Parental leave	Parental leave is an employee benefit that provides paid or unpaid time off work to care for a child or make arrangements for the child"s welfare. Often, the term Parental leave includes maternity, paternity, and adoption leave. In most western countries Parental leave is available for those who have worked for their current employer for a certain period of time.
Corporal punishment	Corporal punishment is the deliberate infliction of pain intended to discipline or reform a wrongdoer or change a person"s bad attitude and/or bad behaviour. The term usually refers to methodically striking the offender with an implement, whether in judicial, domestic, or educational settings.

Corporal punishment may be divided into three main types:

- parental or domestic Corporal punishment, i.e. the spanking of children within the family;
- school Corporal punishment, i.e. of school students by teachers or other school officials;
- judicial Corporal punishment, involving the official caning or whipping of convicted offenders (whether adult or juvenile) by order of a court of law.

The Corporal punishment of minors within the home is lawful in all 50 of the United States and, according to a 2000 survey, it is widely approved by parents. It has been officially outlawed in 24 countries around the world.

Sibling	A Sibling is a brother or a sister; that is, any person who shares at least one of the same parents. In most societies throughout the world, Sibling s usually grow up together and spend a good deal of their childhood with each other. This genetic and physical closeness may be marked by the development of strong emotional associations such as love or enmity.
Mother	A Mother is a biological and/or social female parent of an offspring. Because of the complexity and differences of the social, cultural, and religious definitions and roles, it is challenging to define a Mother in a universally accepted definition. In the case of a mammal such as a human, the biological Mother gestates a fertilized ovum, which is called first an embryo, and then a fetus.

Breastfeeding	Breastfeeding is the feeding of an infant or young child with breast milk directly from human breasts rather than from a baby bottle or other container. Babies have a sucking reflex that enables them to suck and swallow milk. Most mothers can breastfeed for six months or more, without the addition of infant formula or solid food.
Attachment	In Attachment theory psychology, Attachment is a product of the activity of a number of behavioral systems that have proximity to a person, e.g. a mother, as a predictable outcome. The concept of there being an "Attachment" behavior, stage, and process, to which a growing person remains in proximity to another was developed beginning in 1956 by British developmental psychologist John Bowlby. According to Bowlby, the concept of proximity Attachment has its origins in Charles Darwin"s 1856 Origin of Species, which "sees instinctive behavior as the outcome of behavioral structures that are activated by certain conditions and terminated by other conditions", Sigmund Freud"s 1905 Three Essays on the Theory of Sexuality and his 1915 Instincts and their Vicissitudes, which according to Bowlby "postulates part-instincts, differentiates the aim of an instinct, namely the conditions that terminate instinctive behavior, and its function, and notes how labile are the objects towards which any particular sort of instinctive behavior is directed", and Konrad Lorenz"s 1937 theory of imprinting.
Adolescence	Adolescence is a transitional stage of physical and mental human development that occurs between childhood and adulthood. This transition involves biological (i.e. pubertal), social, and psychological changes, though the biological or physiological ones are the easiest to measure objectively. Historically, puberty has been heavily associated with teenagers and the onset of adolescent development.
Infant	An Infant or baby is the term used to refer to the very young offspring of humans and other primates. The term Infant derives from the Latin word infans, meaning "unable to speak." It is typically applied to children between the ages of 1 month and 12 months . However, definitions vary between birth and 3 years of age.
Head Start	Head Start is a program of the United States Department of Health and Human Services that provides comprehensive education, health, nutrition, and parent involvement services to low-income children and their families. Head Start began in 1964 and was later updated by the Head Start Act of 1981. It is the longest-running program to address systemic poverty in the United States.
Childhood	Childhood is a broad term usually applied to the phase of development in humans between infancy and adulthood. In many countries there is an age of majority when Childhood ends and a person legally becomes an adult. The age can range anywhere from 13 to 21, with 18 being the most common.
Day care	Day care or child care is care of a child during the day by a person other than the child"s legal guardians, typically performed by someone outside the child"s immediate family. Day care is typically an ongoing service during specific periods, such as the parents" time at work. The service is known as child care in the United Kingdom and Australia and Day care in North America (although child care also has a broader meaning.)

Adult	The term Adult has at least three distinct meanings. It can indicate a biologically grown or mature person. It may also mean a plant, animal, or person who has reached full growth or alternatively is capable of reproduction, or the classification legal Adult, generally determined as a person who has attained the legally fixed age of majority; as opposed to a minor.
Birth	Birth is the act or process of bearing or bringing forth offspring . The offspring is brought forth from the mother. Different forms of Birth are oviparity, vivipary or ovovivipary.
Learning	Learning is acquiring new knowledge, behaviors, skills, values, preferences or understanding, and may involve synthesizing different types of information. The ability to learn is possessed by humans, animals and some machines. Progress over time tends to follow Learning curves.
Autism	Autism is a brain development disorder characterized by impaired social interaction and communication, and by restricted and repetitive behavior. These signs all begin before a child is three years old. Autism affects many parts of the brain; how this occurs is not understood.
Play	Play is a rite and a quality of mind in engaging with one"s worldview. Play refers to a range of voluntary, intrinsically motivated activities that are normally associated with pleasure and enjoyment. Play may consist of amusing, pretend or imaginary interpersonal and intrapersonal interactions or interplay.
Childbirth	Childbirth is the culmination of a human pregnancy or gestation period with birth of one or more newborn infants from a woman"s uterus. The process of normal human Childbirth is categorized in three stages of labour: the shortening and dilation of the cervix, descent and birth of the infant, and birth of the placenta.. In some cases, Childbirth is achieved through caesarean section, the removal of the neonate through a surgical incision in the abdomen, rather than through vaginal birth.
Intelligence	Intelligence is an umbrella term used to describe a property of the mind that encompasses many related abilities, such as the capacities to reason, to plan, to solve problems, to think abstractly, to comprehend ideas, to use language, and to learn. There are several ways to define Intelligence. In some cases, Intelligence may include traits such as creativity, personality, character, knowledge, or wisdom.
Parenting	Parenting is the process of promoting and supporting the physical, emotional, social, and intellectual development of a child from infancy to adulthood. Parenting refers to the activity of raising a child rather than the biological relationship. In the case of humans, it is usually done by the biological parents of the child in question, although governments and society take a role as well.
Orphan	An Orphan is a child permanently bereaved of his or her parents. Common usage limits the term to children who have lost both parents. In certain animal species where the father typically abandons the mother and young at or prior to birth, the young will be called Orphan s when the mother dies regardless of the condition of the father.

Adolescence	Adolescence is a transitional stage of physical and mental human development that occurs between childhood and adulthood. This transition involves biological (i.e. pubertal), social, and psychological changes, though the biological or physiological ones are the easiest to measure objectively. Historically, puberty has been heavily associated with teenagers and the onset of adolescent development.
Child	A Child (plural: Child ren) is a human being between the stages of birth and puberty. The legal definition of Child generally refers to a minor, otherwise known as a person younger than the age of majority. Child may also describe a relationship with a parent or authority figure, or signify group membership in a clan, tribe, or religion; it can also signify being strongly affected by a specific time, place, or circumstance, as in "a Child of nature" or "a Child of the Sixties." The United Nations Convention on the Rights of the Child defines a Child as "every human being below the age of 18 years unless under the law applicable to the Child majority is attained earlier." Biologically, a Child is anyone in the developmental stage of Child hood, between infancy and adulthood.
Child development	Child development refers to the biological and psychological changes that occur in human beings between birth and the end of adolescence, as the individual progresses from dependency to increasing autonomy. Because these developmental changes may be strongly influenced by genetic factors and events during prenatal life, genetics and prenatal development are usually included as part of the study of Child development. Related terms include "developmental psychology", referring to development throughout the lifespan and "pediatrics", the branch of medicine relating to the care of children.
Childhood	Childhood is a broad term usually applied to the phase of development in humans between infancy and adulthood. In many countries there is an age of majority when Childhood ends and a person legally becomes an adult. The age can range anywhere from 13 to 21, with 18 being the most common.
Early childhood	Early childhood is a stage in human development. It generally includes toddlerhood and some time afterwards. Play age is an unspecific designation approximately within the scope of Early childhood.
Puberty	Puberty refers to the process of physical changes by which a child"s body becomes an adult body capable of reproduction. Puberty is initiated by hormone signals from the brain to the gonads (the ovaries and testes.) In response, the gonads produce a variety of hormones that stimulate the growth, function, or transformation of brain, bones, muscle, skin, breasts, and reproductive organs.
Infant	An Infant or baby is the term used to refer to the very young offspring of humans and other primates. The term Infant derives from the Latin word infans, meaning "unable to speak." It is typically applied to children between the ages of 1 month and 12 months . However, definitions vary between birth and 3 years of age.

Attachment	In Attachment theory psychology, Attachment is a product of the activity of a number of behavioral systems that have proximity to a person, e.g. a mother, as a predictable outcome. The concept of there being an "Attachment" behavior, stage, and process, to which a growing person remains in proximity to another was developed beginning in 1956 by British developmental psychologist John Bowlby. According to Bowlby, the concept of proximity Attachment has its origins in Charles Darwin"s 1856 Origin of Species, which "sees instinctive behavior as the outcome of behavioral structures that are activated by certain conditions and terminated by other conditions", Sigmund Freud"s 1905 Three Essays on the Theory of Sexuality and his 1915 Instincts and their Vicissitudes, which according to Bowlby "postulates part-instincts, differentiates the aim of an instinct, namely the conditions that terminate instinctive behavior, and its function, and notes how labile are the objects towards which any particular sort of instinctive behavior is directed", and Konrad Lorenz"s 1937 theory of imprinting.
Play	Play is a rite and a quality of mind in engaging with one"s worldview. Play refers to a range of voluntary, intrinsically motivated activities that are normally associated with pleasure and enjoyment. Play may consist of amusing, pretend or imaginary interpersonal and intrapersonal interactions or interplay.
Girl	A Girl is any female human from birth through childhood and adolescence to attainment of adulthood. The term may also be used to mean a young woman. The word Girl first appeared during the Middle Ages between 1250 and 1300 CE and came from the Anglo-Saxon words gerle , likely cognate with the Old Low German word gör (sometimes given as kerl.)
Birth	Birth is the act or process of bearing or bringing forth offspring . The offspring is brought forth from the mother. Different forms of Birth are oviparity, vivipary or ovovivipary.
Mental retardation	Mental retardation is a generalized disorder, characterized by subaverage cognitive functioning and deficits in two or more adaptive behaviors with onset before the age of 18. Once focused almost entirely on cognition, the definition now includes both a component relating to mental functioning and one relating to individuals" functional skills in their environment. The term "Mental retardation" is a diagnostic term designed to capture and standardize a group of disconnected categories of mental functioning such as "idiot", "imbecile", and "moron" derived from early IQ tests, which acquired pejorative connotations in popular discourse over time.
Parenting	Parenting is the process of promoting and supporting the physical, emotional, social, and intellectual development of a child from infancy to adulthood. Parenting refers to the activity of raising a child rather than the biological relationship. In the case of humans, it is usually done by the biological parents of the child in question, although governments and society take a role as well.
Breastfeeding	Breastfeeding is the feeding of an infant or young child with breast milk directly from human breasts rather than from a baby bottle or other container. Babies have a sucking reflex that enables them to suck and swallow milk. Most mothers can breastfeed for six months or more, without the addition of infant formula or solid food.

Pregnancy	Pregnancy is the carrying of one or more offspring inside the uterus of a female. In a Pregnancy, there can be multiple gestations, as in the case of twins or triplets. Human Pregnancy is the most studied of all mammalian pregnancies.
Autism	Autism is a brain development disorder characterized by impaired social interaction and communication, and by restricted and repetitive behavior. These signs all begin before a child is three years old. Autism affects many parts of the brain; how this occurs is not understood.
Head Start	Head Start is a program of the United States Department of Health and Human Services that provides comprehensive education, health, nutrition, and parent involvement services to low-income children and their families.
	Head Start began in 1964 and was later updated by the Head Start Act of 1981. It is the longest-running program to address systemic poverty in the United States.
Day care	Day care or child care is care of a child during the day by a person other than the child"s legal guardians, typically performed by someone outside the child"s immediate family. Day care is typically an ongoing service during specific periods, such as the parents" time at work.
	The service is known as child care in the United Kingdom and Australia and Day care in North America (although child care also has a broader meaning.)
Imprinting	Imprinting is the term used in psychology and ethology to describe any kind of phase-sensitive learning (learning occurring at a particular age or a particular life stage) that is rapid and apparently independent of the consequences of behavior. It was first used to describe situations in which an animal or person learns the characteristics of some stimulus, which is therefore said to be "imprinted" onto the subject.
	The best known form of Imprinting is filial Imprinting, in which a young animal learns the characteristics of its parent.
Childbirth	Childbirth is the culmination of a human pregnancy or gestation period with birth of one or more newborn infants from a woman"s uterus. The process of normal human Childbirth is categorized in three stages of labour: the shortening and dilation of the cervix, descent and birth of the infant, and birth of the placenta.. In some cases, Childbirth is achieved through caesarean section, the removal of the neonate through a surgical incision in the abdomen, rather than through vaginal birth.
Father	A Father is defined as a male parent of an offspring. The adjective "paternal" refers to Father parallel to "maternal" for mother.
	The Father child relationship is the defining factor of the Father hood role.
Parent	A Parent is a mother or father; one who sires or gives birth to and/or nurtures and raises an offspring. The different roles of Parent s vary throughout the tree of life, and are especially complex in human culture.
	Like mothers, fathers may be categorised according to their biological, social or legal relationship with the child.

Intelligence	Intelligence is an umbrella term used to describe a property of the mind that encompasses many related abilities, such as the capacities to reason, to plan, to solve problems, to think abstractly, to comprehend ideas, to use language, and to learn. There are several ways to define Intelligence. In some cases, Intelligence may include traits such as creativity, personality, character, knowledge, or wisdom.
Teenage pregnancy	Teenage pregnancy is defined as a teenaged or underage girl (usually within the ages of 13-19) becoming pregnant. The term in everyday speech usually refers to women who have not reached legal adulthood, which varies across the world, who become pregnant. The average age of menarche (first menstrual period) in the United States is 12 years old, though this figure varies by ethnicity and weight, and first ovulation occurs only irregularly until after this.
Parental leave	Parental leave is an employee benefit that provides paid or unpaid time off work to care for a child or make arrangements for the child"s welfare. Often, the term Parental leave includes maternity, paternity, and adoption leave. In most western countries Parental leave is available for those who have worked for their current employer for a certain period of time.
Child support	In family law and government policy, Child support or child maintenance is the ongoing obligation for a periodic payment made directly or indirectly by an ("obligor") to an ("obligee") for the financial care and support of children of a relationship or marriage that has been terminated, or in some cases never existed. Oftentimes, but not always, the obligor is a non-custodial parent. Oftentimes, but not always, the obligee is a custodial parent, caregiver or guardian, or the government.
Mother	A Mother is a biological and/or social female parent of an offspring. Because of the complexity and differences of the social, cultural, and religious definitions and roles, it is challenging to define a Mother in a universally accepted definition. In the case of a mammal such as a human, the biological Mother gestates a fertilized ovum, which is called first an embryo, and then a fetus.

Parenting	Parenting is the process of promoting and supporting the physical, emotional, social, and intellectual development of a child from infancy to adulthood. Parenting refers to the activity of raising a child rather than the biological relationship. In the case of humans, it is usually done by the biological parents of the child in question, although governments and society take a role as well.
Core knowledge perspective	The Core Knowledge Perspective is an evolutionary theory in child development (developmental psychology) that proposes "infants begin life with innate, special-purpose knowledge systems referred to as core domains of thought" There are five core domains of thought, each of which is crucial for survival, which simultaneously prepare us to develop key aspects of early cognition. The five core domains are: physical, numerical, linguistic, psychological, and biological. Physical knowledge is an infant"s comprehension of objects and their effects on one another.
Learning	Learning is acquiring new knowledge, behaviors, skills, values, preferences or understanding, and may involve synthesizing different types of information. The ability to learn is possessed by humans, animals and some machines. Progress over time tends to follow Learning curves.
Theory of cognitive development	The Theory of cognitive development, first developed by Jean Piaget, proposes that there are four distinct, increasingly sophisticated stages of mental representation that children pass through on their way to an adult level of intelligence. The four stages, roughly correlated with age, are as follows: • Sensorimotor period (years 0 to 2) • Preoperational period (years 2 to 7) • Concrete operational period (years 7 to 12) • Formal operational period (years 12 and up) The Sensorimotor Stage is the first of the four stages of cognitive development. "In this stage, infants construct an understanding of the world by coordinating sensory experiences with physical, motoric actions." "Infants gain knowledge of the world from the physical actions they perform on it." "An infant progresses from reflexive, instinctual action at birth to the beginning of symbolic thought toward the end of the stage." "Piaget divided the sensorimotor stage into six sub-stages": "By the end of the sensorimotor period, objects are both separate from the self and permanent." "Object permanence is the understanding that objects continue to exist even when they cannot be seen, heard, or touched." "Acquiring the sense of object permanence is one of the infant"s most important accomplishments, according to Piaget." The Preoperational stage is the second of four stages of cognitive development. By observing sequences of play, Piaget was able to demonstrate that towards the end of the second year, a qualitatively new kind of psychological functioning occurs.
Adult	The term Adult has at least three distinct meanings. It can indicate a biologically grown or mature person. It may also mean a plant, animal, or person who has reached full growth or alternatively is capable of reproduction, or the classification legal Adult, generally determined as a person who has attained the legally fixed age of majority; as opposed to a minor.

Autism	Autism is a brain development disorder characterized by impaired social interaction and communication, and by restricted and repetitive behavior. These signs all begin before a child is three years old. Autism affects many parts of the brain; how this occurs is not understood.
Birth	Birth is the act or process of bearing or bringing forth offspring . The offspring is brought forth from the mother. Different forms of Birth are oviparity, vivipary or ovovivipary.
Play	Play is a rite and a quality of mind in engaging with one"s worldview. Play refers to a range of voluntary, intrinsically motivated activities that are normally associated with pleasure and enjoyment. Play may consist of amusing, pretend or imaginary interpersonal and intrapersonal interactions or interplay.
Early childhood	Early childhood is a stage in human development. It generally includes toddlerhood and some time afterwards. Play age is an unspecific designation approximately within the scope of Early childhood.
Imaginary friends	Imaginary friends are pretend characters often created by children. Imaginary friends often function as tutelaries when they are engaged by the child in play activity. Imaginary friends may exist for the child into adolescence and sometimes adulthood.
Intelligence	Intelligence is an umbrella term used to describe a property of the mind that encompasses many related abilities, such as the capacities to reason, to plan, to solve problems, to think abstractly, to comprehend ideas, to use language, and to learn. There are several ways to define Intelligence. In some cases, Intelligence may include traits such as creativity, personality, character, knowledge, or wisdom.
Attachment	In Attachment theory psychology, Attachment is a product of the activity of a number of behavioral systems that have proximity to a person, e.g. a mother, as a predictable outcome. The concept of there being an "Attachment" behavior, stage, and process, to which a growing person remains in proximity to another was developed beginning in 1956 by British developmental psychologist John Bowlby. According to Bowlby, the concept of proximity Attachment has its origins in Charles Darwin"s 1856 Origin of Species, which "sees instinctive behavior as the outcome of behavioral structures that are activated by certain conditions and terminated by other conditions", Sigmund Freud"s 1905 Three Essays on the Theory of Sexuality and his 1915 Instincts and their Vicissitudes, which according to Bowlby "postulates part-instincts, differentiates the aim of an instinct, namely the conditions that terminate instinctive behavior, and its function, and notes how labile are the objects towards which any particular sort of instinctive behavior is directed", and Konrad Lorenz"s 1937 theory of imprinting.
Conservation	Conservation refers to an ability in logical thinking according to the psychologist Jean Piaget who developed four stages in cognitive development. During third stage, the Concrete operational stage, the child of age 7-11 masters this ability, to logically determine that a certain quantity will remain the same despite adjustment of the container, shape, or apparent size. Conservation earned its name thanks to Jean Piaget, the psychologist responsible for the stages of development.

Centration	Centration is the tendency to focus on one aspect of a situation and neglect others. A term introduced by the Swiss psychologist Jean Piaget (1896-1980) to refer to the tendency of young children to focus attention on only one salient aspect of an object, situation, or problem at a time, to the exclusion of other potentially relevant aspects. A classic example is provided by an experiment first described by Piaget in 1941 in The Child"s Conception of Number in which a child watches while a number of objects are set out in a row and then moved closer together, and the child is asked whether there are now more objects, fewer objects, or the same number of objects.
Adolescence	Adolescence is a transitional stage of physical and mental human development that occurs between childhood and adulthood. This transition involves biological (i.e. pubertal), social, and psychological changes, though the biological or physiological ones are the easiest to measure objectively. Historically, puberty has been heavily associated with teenagers and the onset of adolescent development.
Imaginary audience	The Imaginary audience refers to an egocentric state where an individual imagines and believes that multitudes of people are enthusiastically listening to him or her at all times. Though this state is often exhibited in young adolescence, people of any age may harbor a belief in an Imaginary audience. In extreme cases, belief in an Imaginary audience can lead to paranoia as the sufferer believes he or she is being watched by an invisible audience at all times.
Mental retardation	Mental retardation is a generalized disorder, characterized by subaverage cognitive functioning and deficits in two or more adaptive behaviors with onset before the age of 18. Once focused almost entirely on cognition, the definition now includes both a component relating to mental functioning and one relating to individuals" functional skills in their environment. The term "Mental retardation" is a diagnostic term designed to capture and standardize a group of disconnected categories of mental functioning such as "idiot", "imbecile", and "moron" derived from early IQ tests, which acquired pejorative connotations in popular discourse over time.
Puberty	Puberty refers to the process of physical changes by which a child"s body becomes an adult body capable of reproduction. Puberty is initiated by hormone signals from the brain to the gonads (the ovaries and testes.) In response, the gonads produce a variety of hormones that stimulate the growth, function, or transformation of brain, bones, muscle, skin, breasts, and reproductive organs.
Child	A Child (plural: Child ren) is a human being between the stages of birth and puberty. The legal definition of Child generally refers to a minor, otherwise known as a person younger than the age of majority. Child may also describe a relationship with a parent or authority figure, or signify group membership in a clan, tribe, or religion; it can also signify being strongly affected by a specific time, place, or circumstance, as in "a Child of nature" or "a Child of the Sixties." The United Nations Convention on the Rights of the Child defines a Child as "every human being below the age of 18 years unless under the law applicable to the Child majority is attained earlier." Biologically, a Child is anyone in the developmental stage of Child hood, between infancy and adulthood.

Personal fable	The Personal fable is term coined by David Elkind (1967) that is used in psychology to describe a form of egocentrism normally exhibited during early adolescence, and it is characterized by an over-differentiating of one"s experiences and feelings from others to the point of assuming those experiences are unique from those of others. A person might believe that he is the only one who can experience whatever feelings of joy, horror, misery, or confusion he might encounter.
	Examples of Personal fable can be seen in the following typified assertions made by adolescents:
	<ul><li>"Nobody understands me."</li><li>"My parents just don"t know what I"m going through-- what do they know about what it"s like being a teenager?"</li><li>"You just don"t know how it feels."</li><li>"I just got dumped by the girl I love, and nobody could ever experience the crushing sadness I"m going through."</li></ul>
	Evolving from the same egocentrism and ideas of playing the central part in one"s Personal fable, adolescents may become preoccupied with what others in their peer groups think of them. Because adolescents become so involved with others" opinions, they believe that an imaginary audience is scrutinizing them wherever they are.
Infant	An Infant or baby is the term used to refer to the very young offspring of humans and other primates. The term Infant derives from the Latin word infans, meaning "unable to speak." It is typically applied to children between the ages of 1 month and 12 months . However, definitions vary between birth and 3 years of age.
Day care	Day care or child care is care of a child during the day by a person other than the child"s legal guardians, typically performed by someone outside the child"s immediate family. Day care is typically an ongoing service during specific periods, such as the parents" time at work.
	The service is known as child care in the United Kingdom and Australia and Day care in North America (although child care also has a broader meaning.)
Private speech	Children from two to about seven years old can be observed engaging in Private speech -- speech spoken to oneself for communication, self-guidance, and self-regulation of behavior (Manning, 1991; Vygotsky, 1934/1986; Winsler et al., 1997.) Although it is audible, it is neither intended for nor directed at others (Manning, 1991; Piaget, 1959; White ' Manning, 1994.) Private speech, although first studied by Vygotsky (1934/1986)and Piaget (1959), has received attention from researchers only in the past 30 years (Deniz, 2001a.)
Sibling	A Sibling is a brother or a sister; that is, any person who shares at least one of the same parents. In most societies throughout the world, Sibling s usually grow up together and spend a good deal of their childhood with each other. This genetic and physical closeness may be marked by the development of strong emotional associations such as love or enmity.

Childbirth	Childbirth is the culmination of a human pregnancy or gestation period with birth of one or more newborn infants from a woman"s uterus. The process of normal human Childbirth is categorized in three stages of labour: the shortening and dilation of the cervix, descent and birth of the infant, and birth of the placenta.. In some cases, Childbirth is achieved through caesarean section, the removal of the neonate through a surgical incision in the abdomen, rather than through vaginal birth.
Sibling relationships	Judy Dunn (a leading expert on sibling relationship) in 2007 described three important characteristics of Sibling relationships. Emotional quality of the relatioship: Both intensive postiive and negative emotions are often expressed by siblings toward each other. Many children and adolescents have mixed feelings toward their siblings.
Youth	Youth is the period between childhood and adulthood, described as the period of physical and psychological development from the onset of puberty to maturity and early adulthood. Definitions of the specific age range that constitutes Youth vary. An individual"s actual maturity may not correspond to their chronological age, as immature individuals exist at all ages.
Proportional reasoning	Proportional reasoning Proportionality is a mathematical relation between two quantities. Proportional reasoning is one of the skills a child acquires when progressing from the stage of concrete operations to the stage of formal operations according to Piaget"s theory of intellectual development. "In mathematics and in physics, proportionality is a mathematical relation between two quantities." There are two different views of this "mathematical relation"; one is based on ratios and the other is based on functions.

Core knowledge perspective	The Core Knowledge Perspective is an evolutionary theory in child development (developmental psychology) that proposes "infants begin life with innate, special-purpose knowledge systems referred to as core domains of thought" There are five core domains of thought, each of which is crucial for survival, which simultaneously prepare us to develop key aspects of early cognition. The five core domains are: physical, numerical, linguistic, psychological, and biological. Physical knowledge is an infant"s comprehension of objects and their effects on one another.
Adult	The term Adult has at least three distinct meanings. It can indicate a biologically grown or mature person. It may also mean a plant, animal, or person who has reached full growth or alternatively is capable of reproduction, or the classification legal Adult, generally determined as a person who has attained the legally fixed age of majority; as opposed to a minor.
Conservation	Conservation refers to an ability in logical thinking according to the psychologist Jean Piaget who developed four stages in cognitive development. During third stage, the Concrete operational stage, the child of age 7-11 masters this ability, to logically determine that a certain quantity will remain the same despite adjustment of the container, shape, or apparent size. Conservation earned its name thanks to Jean Piaget, the psychologist responsible for the stages of development.
Infant	An Infant or baby is the term used to refer to the very young offspring of humans and other primates. The term Infant derives from the Latin word infans, meaning "unable to speak." It is typically applied to children between the ages of 1 month and 12 months . However, definitions vary between birth and 3 years of age.
Autism	Autism is a brain development disorder characterized by impaired social interaction and communication, and by restricted and repetitive behavior. These signs all begin before a child is three years old. Autism affects many parts of the brain; how this occurs is not understood.
Adolescence	Adolescence is a transitional stage of physical and mental human development that occurs between childhood and adulthood. This transition involves biological (i.e. pubertal), social, and psychological changes, though the biological or physiological ones are the easiest to measure objectively. Historically, puberty has been heavily associated with teenagers and the onset of adolescent development.
Child	A Child (plural: Child ren) is a human being between the stages of birth and puberty. The legal definition of Child generally refers to a minor, otherwise known as a person younger than the age of majority. Child may also describe a relationship with a parent or authority figure, or signify group membership in a clan, tribe, or religion; it can also signify being strongly affected by a specific time, place, or circumstance, as in "a Child of nature" or "a Child of the Sixties." The United Nations Convention on the Rights of the Child defines a Child as "every human being below the age of 18 years unless under the law applicable to the Child majority is attained earlier." Biologically, a Child is anyone in the developmental stage of Child hood, between infancy and adulthood.

Sign language	Specialized sign language is sometimes used to communicate with infants and toddlers. While infants and toddlers have a desire to communicate their needs and wishes, they lack the ability to do so clearly because the production of speech lags behind cognitive ability in the first months and years of life. Proponents of baby sign language say that this gap between desire to communicate and ability often leads to frustration and tantrums.
Childbirth	Childbirth is the culmination of a human pregnancy or gestation period with birth of one or more newborn infants from a woman"s uterus. The process of normal human Childbirth is categorized in three stages of labour: the shortening and dilation of the cervix, descent and birth of the infant, and birth of the placenta.. In some cases, Childbirth is achieved through caesarean section, the removal of the neonate through a surgical incision in the abdomen, rather than through vaginal birth.
Learning	Learning is acquiring new knowledge, behaviors, skills, values, preferences or understanding, and may involve synthesizing different types of information. The ability to learn is possessed by humans, animals and some machines. Progress over time tends to follow Learning curves.
Theory of cognitive development	The Theory of cognitive development, first developed by Jean Piaget, proposes that there are four distinct, increasingly sophisticated stages of mental representation that children pass through on their way to an adult level of intelligence. The four stages, roughly correlated with age, are as follows: • Sensorimotor period (years 0 to 2) • Preoperational period (years 2 to 7) • Concrete operational period (years 7 to 12) • Formal operational period (years 12 and up) The Sensorimotor Stage is the first of the four stages of cognitive development. "In this stage, infants construct an understanding of the world by coordinating sensory experiences with physical, motoric actions." "Infants gain knowledge of the world from the physical actions they perform on it." "An infant progresses from reflexive, instinctual action at birth to the beginning of symbolic thought toward the end of the stage." "Piaget divided the sensorimotor stage into six sub-stages": "By the end of the sensorimotor period, objects are both separate from the self and permanent." "Object permanence is the understanding that objects continue to exist even when they cannot be seen, heard, or touched." "Acquiring the sense of object permanence is one of the infant"s most important accomplishments, according to Piaget." The Preoperational stage is the second of four stages of cognitive development. By observing sequences of play, Piaget was able to demonstrate that towards the end of the second year, a qualitatively new kind of psychological functioning occurs.
Play	Play is a rite and a quality of mind in engaging with one"s worldview. Play refers to a range of voluntary, intrinsically motivated activities that are normally associated with pleasure and enjoyment. Play may consist of amusing, pretend or imaginary interpersonal and intrapersonal interactions or interplay.

Head Start

Head Start is a program of the United States Department of Health and Human Services that provides comprehensive education, health, nutrition, and parent involvement services to low-income children and their families.

Head Start began in 1964 and was later updated by the Head Start Act of 1981. It is the longest-running program to address systemic poverty in the United States.

Intelligence

Intelligence is an umbrella term used to describe a property of the mind that encompasses many related abilities, such as the capacities to reason, to plan, to solve problems, to think abstractly, to comprehend ideas, to use language, and to learn. There are several ways to define Intelligence. In some cases, Intelligence may include traits such as creativity, personality, character, knowledge, or wisdom.

Attachment

In Attachment theory psychology, Attachment is a product of the activity of a number of behavioral systems that have proximity to a person, e.g. a mother, as a predictable outcome. The concept of there being an "Attachment" behavior, stage, and process, to which a growing person remains in proximity to another was developed beginning in 1956 by British developmental psychologist John Bowlby. According to Bowlby, the concept of proximity Attachment has its origins in Charles Darwin"s 1856 Origin of Species, which "sees instinctive behavior as the outcome of behavioral structures that are activated by certain conditions and terminated by other conditions", Sigmund Freud"s 1905 Three Essays on the Theory of Sexuality and his 1915 Instincts and their Vicissitudes, which according to Bowlby "postulates part-instincts, differentiates the aim of an instinct, namely the conditions that terminate instinctive behavior, and its function, and notes how labile are the objects towards which any particular sort of instinctive behavior is directed", and Konrad Lorenz"s 1937 theory of imprinting.

Childhood

Childhood is a broad term usually applied to the phase of development in humans between infancy and adulthood.

In many countries there is an age of majority when Childhood ends and a person legally becomes an adult. The age can range anywhere from 13 to 21, with 18 being the most common.

Early childhood

Early childhood is a stage in human development. It generally includes toddlerhood and some time afterwards. Play age is an unspecific designation approximately within the scope of Early childhood.

Phonics

Phonics refers to a method for teaching speakers of English to read and write that language. Phonics involves teaching how to connect the sounds of spoken English with letters or groups of letters and teaching them to blend the sounds of letters together to produce approximate pronunciations of unknown words.

Phonics is a widely used method of teaching to read and decode words, although it is not without controversy

Infant	An Infant or baby is the term used to refer to the very young offspring of humans and other primates. The term Infant derives from the Latin word infans, meaning "unable to speak." It is typically applied to children between the ages of 1 month and 12 months . However, definitions vary between birth and 3 years of age.
Intelligence	Intelligence is an umbrella term used to describe a property of the mind that encompasses many related abilities, such as the capacities to reason, to plan, to solve problems, to think abstractly, to comprehend ideas, to use language, and to learn. There are several ways to define Intelligence. In some cases, Intelligence may include traits such as creativity, personality, character, knowledge, or wisdom.
Girl	A Girl is any female human from birth through childhood and adolescence to attainment of adulthood. The term may also be used to mean a young woman. The word Girl first appeared during the Middle Ages between 1250 and 1300 CE and came from the Anglo-Saxon words gerle , likely cognate with the Old Low German word gör (sometimes given as kerl.)
Youth	Youth is the period between childhood and adulthood, described as the period of physical and psychological development from the onset of puberty to maturity and early adulthood. Definitions of the specific age range that constitutes Youth vary. An individual"s actual maturity may not correspond to their chronological age, as immature individuals exist at all ages.
Core knowledge perspective	The Core Knowledge Perspective is an evolutionary theory in child development (developmental psychology) that proposes "infants begin life with innate, special-purpose knowledge systems referred to as core domains of thought" There are five core domains of thought, each of which is crucial for survival, which simultaneously prepare us to develop key aspects of early cognition. The five core domains are: physical, numerical, linguistic, psychological, and biological. Physical knowledge is an infant"s comprehension of objects and their effects on one another.
Childhood	Childhood is a broad term usually applied to the phase of development in humans between infancy and adulthood. In many countries there is an age of majority when Childhood ends and a person legally becomes an adult. The age can range anywhere from 13 to 21, with 18 being the most common.
Early childhood	Early childhood is a stage in human development. It generally includes toddlerhood and some time afterwards. Play age is an unspecific designation approximately within the scope of Early childhood.
Head Start	Head Start is a program of the United States Department of Health and Human Services that provides comprehensive education, health, nutrition, and parent involvement services to low-income children and their families. Head Start began in 1964 and was later updated by the Head Start Act of 1981. It is the longest-running program to address systemic poverty in the United States.
Sibling	A Sibling is a brother or a sister; that is, any person who shares at least one of the same parents.

In most societies throughout the world, Sibling s usually grow up together and spend a good deal of their childhood with each other. This genetic and physical closeness may be marked by the development of strong emotional associations such as love or enmity.

Theory of cognitive development	The Theory of cognitive development, first developed by Jean Piaget, proposes that there are four distinct, increasingly sophisticated stages of mental representation that children pass through on their way to an adult level of intelligence. The four stages, roughly correlated with age, are as follows: • Sensorimotor period (years 0 to 2) • Preoperational period (years 2 to 7) • Concrete operational period (years 7 to 12) • Formal operational period (years 12 and up) The Sensorimotor Stage is the first of the four stages of cognitive development. "In this stage, infants construct an understanding of the world by coordinating sensory experiences with physical, motoric actions." "Infants gain knowledge of the world from the physical actions they perform on it." "An infant progresses from reflexive, instinctual action at birth to the beginning of symbolic thought toward the end of the stage." "Piaget divided the sensorimotor stage into six sub-stages": "By the end of the sensorimotor period, objects are both separate from the self and permanent." "Object permanence is the understanding that objects continue to exist even when they cannot be seen, heard, or touched." "Acquiring the sense of object permanence is one of the infant"s most important accomplishments, according to Piaget." The Preoperational stage is the second of four stages of cognitive development. By observing sequences of play, Piaget was able to demonstrate that towards the end of the second year, a qualitatively new kind of psychological functioning occurs.
Child	A Child (plural: Child ren) is a human being between the stages of birth and puberty. The legal definition of Child generally refers to a minor, otherwise known as a person younger than the age of majority. Child may also describe a relationship with a parent or authority figure, or signify group membership in a clan, tribe, or religion; it can also signify being strongly affected by a specific time, place, or circumstance, as in "a Child of nature" or "a Child of the Sixties." The United Nations Convention on the Rights of the Child defines a Child as "every human being below the age of 18 years unless under the law applicable to the Child majority is attained earlier." Biologically, a Child is anyone in the developmental stage of Child hood, between infancy and adulthood.
Kindergarten	In each state of Australia, Kindergarten means something slightly different. In New South Wales and the Australian Capital Territory, it is the first year of primary school. In Victoria, Kindergarten is a form of preschool and may be referred to interchangeably as preschool or Kindergarten.
Learning	Learning is acquiring new knowledge, behaviors, skills, values, preferences or understanding, and may involve synthesizing different types of information. The ability to learn is possessed by humans, animals and some machines. Progress over time tends to follow Learning curves.

56

Adult	The term Adult has at least three distinct meanings. It can indicate a biologically grown or mature person. It may also mean a plant, animal, or person who has reached full growth or alternatively is capable of reproduction, or the classification legal Adult, generally determined as a person who has attained the legally fixed age of majority; as opposed to a minor.
Attachment	In Attachment theory psychology, Attachment is a product of the activity of a number of behavioral systems that have proximity to a person, e.g. a mother, as a predictable outcome. The concept of there being an "Attachment" behavior, stage, and process, to which a growing person remains in proximity to another was developed beginning in 1956 by British developmental psychologist John Bowlby. According to Bowlby, the concept of proximity Attachment has its origins in Charles Darwin"s 1856 Origin of Species, which "sees instinctive behavior as the outcome of behavioral structures that are activated by certain conditions and terminated by other conditions", Sigmund Freud"s 1905 Three Essays on the Theory of Sexuality and his 1915 Instincts and their Vicissitudes, which according to Bowlby "postulates part-instincts, differentiates the aim of an instinct, namely the conditions that terminate instinctive behavior, and its function, and notes how labile are the objects towards which any particular sort of instinctive behavior is directed", and Konrad Lorenz"s 1937 theory of imprinting.
Autism	Autism is a brain development disorder characterized by impaired social interaction and communication, and by restricted and repetitive behavior. These signs all begin before a child is three years old. Autism affects many parts of the brain; how this occurs is not understood.
Sign Language	Specialized sign language is sometimes used to communicate with infants and toddlers. While infants and toddlers have a desire to communicate their needs and wishes, they lack the ability to do so clearly because the production of speech lags behind cognitive ability in the first months and years of life. Proponents of baby sign language say that this gap between desire to communicate and ability often leads to frustration and tantrums.
Parenting	Parenting is the process of promoting and supporting the physical, emotional, social, and intellectual development of a child from infancy to adulthood. Parenting refers to the activity of raising a child rather than the biological relationship. In the case of humans, it is usually done by the biological parents of the child in question, although governments and society take a role as well.
Youth	Youth is the period between childhood and adulthood, described as the period of physical and psychological development from the onset of puberty to maturity and early adulthood. Definitions of the specific age range that constitutes Youth vary. An individual"s actual maturity may not correspond to their chronological age, as immature individuals exist at all ages.
Mental retardation	Mental retardation is a generalized disorder, characterized by subaverage cognitive functioning and deficits in two or more adaptive behaviors with onset before the age of 18. Once focused almost entirely on cognition, the definition now includes both a component relating to mental functioning and one relating to individuals" functional skills in their environment. The term "Mental retardation" is a diagnostic term designed to capture and standardize a group of disconnected categories of mental functioning such as "idiot", "imbecile", and "moron" derived from early IQ tests, which acquired pejorative connotations in popular discourse over time.

101

Infant	An Infant or baby is the term used to refer to the very young offspring of humans and other primates. The term Infant derives from the Latin word infans, meaning "unable to speak." It is typically applied to children between the ages of 1 month and 12 months . However, definitions vary between birth and 3 years of age.
Learning	Learning is acquiring new knowledge, behaviors, skills, values, preferences or understanding, and may involve synthesizing different types of information. The ability to learn is possessed by humans, animals and some machines. Progress over time tends to follow Learning curves.
Speech perception	Speech perception refers to the processes by which humans are able to interpret and understand the sounds used in language. The study of Speech perception is closely linked to the fields of phonetics and phonology in linguistics and cognitive psychology and perception in psychology. Research in Speech perception seeks to understand how human listeners recognize speech sounds and use this information to understand spoken language.
Juvenile delinquency	Juvenile delinquency refers to criminal acts performed by juveniles. Most legal systems prescribe specific procedures for dealing with juveniles, such as juvenile detention centers. There are a multitude of different theories on the causes of crime, most if not all of which can be applied to the causes of youth crime.
Play	Play is a rite and a quality of mind in engaging with one"s worldview. Play refers to a range of voluntary, intrinsically motivated activities that are normally associated with pleasure and enjoyment. Play may consist of amusing, pretend or imaginary interpersonal and intrapersonal interactions or interplay.
Adolescence	Adolescence is a transitional stage of physical and mental human development that occurs between childhood and adulthood. This transition involves biological (i.e. pubertal), social, and psychological changes, though the biological or physiological ones are the easiest to measure objectively. Historically, puberty has been heavily associated with teenagers and the onset of adolescent development.
Child	A Child (plural: Child ren) is a human being between the stages of birth and puberty. The legal definition of Child generally refers to a minor, otherwise known as a person younger than the age of majority. Child may also describe a relationship with a parent or authority figure, or signify group membership in a clan, tribe, or religion; it can also signify being strongly affected by a specific time, place, or circumstance, as in "a Child of nature" or "a Child of the Sixties." The United Nations Convention on the Rights of the Child defines a Child as "every human being below the age of 18 years unless under the law applicable to the Child majority is attained earlier." Biologically, a Child is anyone in the developmental stage of Child hood, between infancy and adulthood.
Parent	A Parent is a mother or father; one who sires or gives birth to and/or nurtures and raises an offspring. The different roles of Parent s vary throughout the tree of life, and are especially complex in human culture.

Like mothers, fathers may be categorised according to their biological, social or legal relationship with the child.

Intelligence

Intelligence is an umbrella term used to describe a property of the mind that encompasses many related abilities, such as the capacities to reason, to plan, to solve problems, to think abstractly, to comprehend ideas, to use language, and to learn. There are several ways to define Intelligence. In some cases, Intelligence may include traits such as creativity, personality, character, knowledge, or wisdom.

Sibling

A Sibling is a brother or a sister; that is, any person who shares at least one of the same parents. In most societies throughout the world, Sibling s usually grow up together and spend a good deal of their childhood with each other. This genetic and physical closeness may be marked by the development of strong emotional associations such as love or enmity.

Sibling relationships

Judy Dunn (a leading expert on sibling relationship) in 2007 described three important characteristics of Sibling relationships. Emotional quality of the relatioship: Both intensive postiive and negative emotions are often expressed by siblings toward each other. Many children and adolescents have mixed feelings toward their siblings.

| Attachment | In Attachment theory psychology, Attachment is a product of the activity of a number of behavioral systems that have proximity to a person, e.g. a mother, as a predictable outcome. The concept of there being an "Attachment" behavior, stage, and process, to which a growing person remains in proximity to another was developed beginning in 1956 by British developmental psychologist John Bowlby. According to Bowlby, the concept of proximity Attachment has its origins in Charles Darwin"s 1856 Origin of Species, which "sees instinctive behavior as the outcome of behavioral structures that are activated by certain conditions and terminated by other conditions", Sigmund Freud"s 1905 Three Essays on the Theory of Sexuality and his 1915 Instincts and their Vicissitudes, which according to Bowlby "postulates part-instincts, differentiates the aim of an instinct, namely the conditions that terminate instinctive behavior, and its function, and notes how labile are the objects towards which any particular sort of instinctive behavior is directed", and Konrad Lorenz"s 1937 theory of imprinting. |

| Child | A Child (plural: Child ren) is a human being between the stages of birth and puberty. The legal definition of Child generally refers to a minor, otherwise known as a person younger than the age of majority. Child may also describe a relationship with a parent or authority figure, or signify group membership in a clan, tribe, or religion; it can also signify being strongly affected by a specific time, place, or circumstance, as in "a Child of nature" or "a Child of the Sixties." |
| | The United Nations Convention on the Rights of the Child defines a Child as "every human being below the age of 18 years unless under the law applicable to the Child majority is attained earlier." Biologically, a Child is anyone in the developmental stage of Child hood, between infancy and adulthood. |

Ecological systems theory	Ecological Systems Theory specifies four types of nested environmental systems, with bi-directional influences within and between the systems.
	The theory was developed by Urie Bronfenbrenner, generally regarded as one of the world"s leading scholars in the field of developmental psychology.
	The four systems:

- Microsystem: Immediate environments
- Mesosystem: A system comprising connections between immediate environments
- Exosystem: External environmental settings which only indirectly affect development
- Macrosystem: The larger cultural context

Later, a fifth system was added:

- Chronosystem: The patterning of environmental events and transitions over the course of life.

The person"s own biology may be considered part of the microsystem; thus the theory has recently sometimes been called "Bio-Ecological Systems Theory."

Per this theoretical construction, each system contains roles, norms and rules which may shape psychological development.

Adolescence	Adolescence is a transitional stage of physical and mental human development that occurs between childhood and adulthood. This transition involves biological (i.e. pubertal), social, and psychological changes, though the biological or physiological ones are the easiest to measure objectively. Historically, puberty has been heavily associated with teenagers and the onset of adolescent development.
Breastfeeding	Breastfeeding is the feeding of an infant or young child with breast milk directly from human breasts rather than from a baby bottle or other container. Babies have a sucking reflex that enables them to suck and swallow milk. Most mothers can breastfeed for six months or more, without the addition of infant formula or solid food.
Caregiver	Carer (UK, NZ, Australian usage) and Caregiver are words normally used to refer to unpaid relatives or friends who support people with disabilities. The words may be prefixed with "Family" "Spousal" or "Child" to distinguish between different care situations. Terms such as "Voluntary Caregiver" and "Informal carer" are also used occasionally, but these terms have been criticized by carers as misnomers because they are perceived as belittling the huge impact that caring may have on an individual"s life, the lack of realistic alternatives, and the degree of perceived duty of care felt by many relatives.
Childbirth	Childbirth is the culmination of a human pregnancy or gestation period with birth of one or more newborn infants from a woman"s uterus. The process of normal human Childbirth is categorized in three stages of labour: the shortening and dilation of the cervix, descent and birth of the infant, and birth of the placenta.. In some cases, Childbirth is achieved through caesarean section, the removal of the neonate through a surgical incision in the abdomen, rather than through vaginal birth.
Infant	An Infant or baby is the term used to refer to the very young offspring of humans and other primates. The term Infant derives from the Latin word infans, meaning "unable to speak." It is typically applied to children between the ages of 1 month and 12 months . However, definitions vary between birth and 3 years of age.
Intelligence	Intelligence is an umbrella term used to describe a property of the mind that encompasses many related abilities, such as the capacities to reason, to plan, to solve problems, to think abstractly, to comprehend ideas, to use language, and to learn. There are several ways to define Intelligence. In some cases, Intelligence may include traits such as creativity, personality, character, knowledge, or wisdom.
Orphan	An Orphan is a child permanently bereaved of his or her parents. Common usage limits the term to children who have lost both parents. In certain animal species where the father typically abandons the mother and young at or prior to birth, the young will be called Orphan s when the mother dies regardless of the condition of the father.
Postpartum depression	Postpartum depression is a form of clinical depression which can affect women, and less frequently men, after childbirth. Studies report prevalence rates among women from 5% to 25%, but methodological differences among the studies make the actual prevalence rate unclear.

	PPE is caused by sleep deprivations coupled with hormonal changes in the woman"s body shortly after giving birth and may be mild or severe.
Mother	A Mother is a biological and/or social female parent of an offspring. Because of the complexity and differences of the social, cultural, and religious definitions and roles, it is challenging to define a Mother in a universally accepted definition. In the case of a mammal such as a human, the biological Mother gestates a fertilized ovum, which is called first an embryo, and then a fetus.
Stranger anxiety	Stranger anxiety is a form of distress that children experience when exposed to people unfamiliar to them. Symptoms may vary, but include: getting very quiet and staring at the stranger, verbally protesting by cries or other vocalizations and/or hiding behind a parent. Stranger anxiety is a typical and therefore normal part of the developmental sequence that most children experience.
Display rules	Display rules are a social group"s informal norms about when, where, and how one should express emotions. Expressions of emotions vary to a great degree and hold significant meaning with great value of determining ones cultural and social identity. Display rules identify these expressions to a precise situation in a suitable context.
Childhood	Childhood is a broad term usually applied to the phase of development in humans between infancy and adulthood. In many countries there is an age of majority when Childhood ends and a person legally becomes an adult. The age can range anywhere from 13 to 21, with 18 being the most common.
Early childhood	Early childhood is a stage in human development. It generally includes toddlerhood and some time afterwards. Play age is an unspecific designation approximately within the scope of Early childhood.
Parent	A Parent is a mother or father; one who sires or gives birth to and/or nurtures and raises an offspring. The different roles of Parent s vary throughout the tree of life, and are especially complex in human culture. Like mothers, fathers may be categorised according to their biological, social or legal relationship with the child.
Learning	Learning is acquiring new knowledge, behaviors, skills, values, preferences or understanding, and may involve synthesizing different types of information. The ability to learn is possessed by humans, animals and some machines. Progress over time tends to follow Learning curves.
Adult	The term Adult has at least three distinct meanings. It can indicate a biologically grown or mature person. It may also mean a plant, animal, or person who has reached full growth or alternatively is capable of reproduction, or the classification legal Adult, generally determined as a person who has attained the legally fixed age of majority; as opposed to a minor.

Play	Play is a rite and a quality of mind in engaging with one"s worldview. Play refers to a range of voluntary, intrinsically motivated activities that are normally associated with pleasure and enjoyment. Play may consist of amusing, pretend or imaginary interpersonal and intrapersonal interactions or interplay.
Theory of cognitive development	The Theory of cognitive development, first developed by Jean Piaget, proposes that there are four distinct, increasingly sophisticated stages of mental representation that children pass through on their way to an adult level of intelligence. The four stages, roughly correlated with age, are as follows: • Sensorimotor period (years 0 to 2) • Preoperational period (years 2 to 7) • Concrete operational period (years 7 to 12) • Formal operational period (years 12 and up) The Sensorimotor Stage is the first of the four stages of cognitive development. "In this stage, infants construct an understanding of the world by coordinating sensory experiences with physical, motoric actions." "Infants gain knowledge of the world from the physical actions they perform on it." "An infant progresses from reflexive, instinctual action at birth to the beginning of symbolic thought toward the end of the stage." "Piaget divided the sensorimotor stage into six sub-stages": "By the end of the sensorimotor period, objects are both separate from the self and permanent." "Object permanence is the understanding that objects continue to exist even when they cannot be seen, heard, or touched." "Acquiring the sense of object permanence is one of the infant"s most important accomplishments, according to Piaget." The Preoperational stage is the second of four stages of cognitive development. By observing sequences of play, Piaget was able to demonstrate that towards the end of the second year, a qualitatively new kind of psychological functioning occurs.
Emerging adulthood	Emerging adulthood is a phase of the life span between adolescence and full-fledged adulthood, proposed by Jeffrey Arnett in a 2000 article in the American Psychologist (summary of article 469.)
Maternal deprivation	The term Maternal deprivation is a catch-phrase summarising the early work of psychiatrist and psychoanalyst, John Bowlby on the effects of separating infants and young children from their mother (or mother-substitute) although the effect of loss of the mother on the developing child had been considered earlier by Freud and other theorists. Bowlby"s work on delinquent and affectionless children and the effects of hospital and institutional care lead to his being commissioned to write the World Health Organisation"s report on the mental health of homeless children in post-war Europe whilst he was head of the Department for Children and Parents at the Tavistock Clinic in London after World War II. The result was the monograph Maternal Care and Mental Health published in 1951, which sets out the Maternal deprivation hypothesis. Bowlby drew together such empirical evidence as existed at the time from across Europe and the USA, including Spitz (1946) and Goldfarb (1943, 1945.)
Girl	A Girl is any female human from birth through childhood and adolescence to attainment of adulthood. The term may also be used to mean a young woman.

	The word Girl first appeared during the Middle Ages between 1250 and 1300 CE and came from the Anglo-Saxon words gerle , likely cognate with the Old Low German word gör (sometimes given as kerl.)
Attachment theory	Attachment theory, originating in the work of psychiatrist and psychoanalyst John Bowlby, is a psychological, evolutionary and ethological theory that provides a descriptive and explanatory framework for understanding interpersonal relationships between human beings. Attachment theorists consider children to have a need for a secure relationship with adult caregivers, without which normal social and emotional development will not occur. Within Attachment theory it is proposed that infant behaviour associated with attachment is primarily a process of proximity seeking to an identified attachment figure in stressful situations, for the purpose of survival.
Imprinting	Imprinting is the term used in psychology and ethology to describe any kind of phase-sensitive learning (learning occurring at a particular age or a particular life stage) that is rapid and apparently independent of the consequences of behavior. It was first used to describe situations in which an animal or person learns the characteristics of some stimulus, which is therefore said to be "imprinted" onto the subject. The best known form of Imprinting is filial Imprinting, in which a young animal learns the characteristics of its parent.
Parenting	Parenting is the process of promoting and supporting the physical, emotional, social, and intellectual development of a child from infancy to adulthood. Parenting refers to the activity of raising a child rather than the biological relationship. In the case of humans, it is usually done by the biological parents of the child in question, although governments and society take a role as well.
Birth	Birth is the act or process of bearing or bringing forth offspring . The offspring is brought forth from the mother. Different forms of Birth are oviparity, vivipary or ovovivipary.
Birth order	Birth order is defined as a person"s rank by age among his or her siblings. Birth order is often believed to have a profound and lasting effect on psychological development. This assertion has been repeatedly challenged by researchers, yet Birth order continues to have a strong presence in pop psychology and popular culture. Alfred Adler (1870-1937), an Austrian psychiatrist, and a contemporary of Sigmund Freud and Carl Jung, was one of the first theorists to suggest that Birth order influences personality.
Father	A Father is defined as a male parent of an offspring. The adjective "paternal" refers to Father parallel to "maternal" for mother. The Father child relationship is the defining factor of the Father hood role.

101

Developmental
disability

Developmental disability is a term used to describe life-long, disabilities attributable to mental and/or physical or combination of mental and physical impairments, manifested prior to age 18. The term is used most commonly in the United States to refer to disabilities affecting daily functioning in three or more of the following areas:

- capacity for independent living
- economic self-sufficiency
- learning
- mobility
- receptive and expressive language
- self-care
- self-direction

The term first appeared in U.S. law in 1970, when Congress used the term to describe the population of individuals who had historically been placed in state institutions, in its effort to improve conditions in these dehumanizing facilities (P.L. 91-517, "The Developmental Disabilities Services and Facilities Construction Act of 1970".) The law has since been amended many times, and now calls for the full community inclusion and self-determination of people with developmental disabilities (P.L. 106-402.) Frequently, people with mental retardation, cerebral palsy, autism spectrum disorder, various genetic and chromosomal disorders such as Down syndrome and Fragile X syndrome, and Fetal Alcohol Spectrum Disorder are described as having developmental disabilities.

Attachment	In Attachment theory psychology, Attachment is a product of the activity of a number of behavioral systems that have proximity to a person, e.g. a mother, as a predictable outcome. The concept of there being an "Attachment" behavior, stage, and process, to which a growing person remains in proximity to another was developed beginning in 1956 by British developmental psychologist John Bowlby. According to Bowlby, the concept of proximity Attachment has its origins in Charles Darwin"s 1856 Origin of Species, which "sees instinctive behavior as the outcome of behavioral structures that are activated by certain conditions and terminated by other conditions", Sigmund Freud"s 1905 Three Essays on the Theory of Sexuality and his 1915 Instincts and their Vicissitudes, which according to Bowlby "postulates part-instincts, differentiates the aim of an instinct, namely the conditions that terminate instinctive behavior, and its function, and notes how labile are the objects towards which any particular sort of instinctive behavior is directed", and Konrad Lorenz"s 1937 theory of imprinting.
Autism	Autism is a brain development disorder characterized by impaired social interaction and communication, and by restricted and repetitive behavior. These signs all begin before a child is three years old. Autism affects many parts of the brain; how this occurs is not understood.
Parenting	Parenting is the process of promoting and supporting the physical, emotional, social, and intellectual development of a child from infancy to adulthood. Parenting refers to the activity of raising a child rather than the biological relationship. In the case of humans, it is usually done by the biological parents of the child in question, although governments and society take a role as well.
Parenting style	Parenting style is a psychological construct representing standard strategies parents use in raising their children. One of the best known theories of Parenting style was developed by Diana Baumrind. "Baumrind believes that parents should be neither punitive nor aloof." Rather, they should develop rules for their children and be affectionate with them.
Child	A Child (plural: Child ren) is a human being between the stages of birth and puberty. The legal definition of Child generally refers to a minor, otherwise known as a person younger than the age of majority. Child may also describe a relationship with a parent or authority figure, or signify group membership in a clan, tribe, or religion; it can also signify being strongly affected by a specific time, place, or circumstance, as in "a Child of nature" or "a Child of the Sixties." The United Nations Convention on the Rights of the Child defines a Child as "every human being below the age of 18 years unless under the law applicable to the Child majority is attained earlier." Biologically, a Child is anyone in the developmental stage of Child hood, between infancy and adulthood.
Theory of cognitive development	The Theory of cognitive development, first developed by Jean Piaget, proposes that there are four distinct, increasingly sophisticated stages of mental representation that children pass through on their way to an adult level of intelligence.

The four stages, roughly correlated with age, are as follows:

- Sensorimotor period (years 0 to 2)
- Preoperational period (years 2 to 7)
- Concrete operational period (years 7 to 12)
- Formal operational period (years 12 and up)

The Sensorimotor Stage is the first of the four stages of cognitive development. "In this stage, infants construct an understanding of the world by coordinating sensory experiences with physical, motoric actions." "Infants gain knowledge of the world from the physical actions they perform on it." "An infant progresses from reflexive, instinctual action at birth to the beginning of symbolic thought toward the end of the stage." "Piaget divided the sensorimotor stage into six sub-stages":

"By the end of the sensorimotor period, objects are both separate from the self and permanent." "Object permanence is the understanding that objects continue to exist even when they cannot be seen, heard, or touched." "Acquiring the sense of object permanence is one of the infant"s most important accomplishments, according to Piaget."

The Preoperational stage is the second of four stages of cognitive development. By observing sequences of play, Piaget was able to demonstrate that towards the end of the second year, a qualitatively new kind of psychological functioning occurs.

Intelligence	Intelligence is an umbrella term used to describe a property of the mind that encompasses many related abilities, such as the capacities to reason, to plan, to solve problems, to think abstractly, to comprehend ideas, to use language, and to learn. There are several ways to define Intelligence. In some cases, Intelligence may include traits such as creativity, personality, character, knowledge, or wisdom.
Sibling	A Sibling is a brother or a sister; that is, any person who shares at least one of the same parents. In most societies throughout the world, Sibling s usually grow up together and spend a good deal of their childhood with each other. This genetic and physical closeness may be marked by the development of strong emotional associations such as love or enmity.
Sibling relationships	Judy Dunn (a leading expert on sibling relationship) in 2007 described three important characteristics of Sibling relationships. Emotional quality of the relatioship: Both intensive postiive and negative emotions are often expressed by siblings toward each other. Many children and adolescents have mixed feelings toward their siblings.
Adolescence	Adolescence is a transitional stage of physical and mental human development that occurs between childhood and adulthood. This transition involves biological (i.e. pubertal), social, and psychological changes, though the biological or physiological ones are the easiest to measure objectively. Historically, puberty has been heavily associated with teenagers and the onset of adolescent development.
Childhood	Childhood is a broad term usually applied to the phase of development in humans between infancy and adulthood.

	In many countries there is an age of majority when Childhood ends and a person legally becomes an adult. The age can range anywhere from 13 to 21, with 18 being the most common.
Early childhood	Early childhood is a stage in human development. It generally includes toddlerhood and some time afterwards. Play age is an unspecific designation approximately within the scope of Early childhood.
Conservation	Conservation refers to an ability in logical thinking according to the psychologist Jean Piaget who developed four stages in cognitive development. During third stage, the Concrete operational stage, the child of age 7-11 masters this ability, to logically determine that a certain quantity will remain the same despite adjustment of the container, shape, or apparent size. Conservation earned its name thanks to Jean Piaget, the psychologist responsible for the stages of development.
Play	Play is a rite and a quality of mind in engaging with one"s worldview. Play refers to a range of voluntary, intrinsically motivated activities that are normally associated with pleasure and enjoyment. Play may consist of amusing, pretend or imaginary interpersonal and intrapersonal interactions or interplay.
Emerging adulthood	Emerging adulthood is a phase of the life span between adolescence and full-fledged adulthood, proposed by Jeffrey Arnett in a 2000 article in the American Psychologist (summary of article 469.)
Marriage	Marriage is a social union of individuals that creates kinship. This union may also be called matrimony, while the ceremony that marks its beginning is usually called a wedding and the married status created is sometimes called wedlock. Marriage is an institution in which interpersonal relationships (usually intimate and sexual) are acknowledged by a variety of ways, depending on the culture or demographic.
Learning	Learning is acquiring new knowledge, behaviors, skills, values, preferences or understanding, and may involve synthesizing different types of information. The ability to learn is possessed by humans, animals and some machines. Progress over time tends to follow Learning curves.
Head Start	Head Start is a program of the United States Department of Health and Human Services that provides comprehensive education, health, nutrition, and parent involvement services to low-income children and their families. Head Start began in 1964 and was later updated by the Head Start Act of 1981. It is the longest-running program to address systemic poverty in the United States.
Youth	Youth is the period between childhood and adulthood, described as the period of physical and psychological development from the onset of puberty to maturity and early adulthood. Definitions of the specific age range that constitutes Youth vary. An individual"s actual maturity may not correspond to their chronological age, as immature individuals exist at all ages.

Imaginary audience	The Imaginary audience refers to an egocentric state where an individual imagines and believes that multitudes of people are enthusiastically listening to him or her at all times. Though this state is often exhibited in young adolescence, people of any age may harbor a belief in an Imaginary audience. In extreme cases, belief in an Imaginary audience can lead to paranoia as the sufferer believes he or she is being watched by an invisible audience at all times.
Ecological systems theory	Ecological Systems Theory specifies four types of nested environmental systems, with bi-directional influences within and between the systems. The theory was developed by Urie Bronfenbrenner, generally regarded as one of the world"s leading scholars in the field of developmental psychology. The four systems: <ul><li>Microsystem: Immediate environments</li><li>Mesosystem: A system comprising connections between immediate environments</li><li>Exosystem: External environmental settings which only indirectly affect development</li><li>Macrosystem: The larger cultural context</li></ul>Later, a fifth system was added: <ul><li>Chronosystem: The patterning of environmental events and transitions over the course of life.</li></ul>The person"s own biology may be considered part of the microsystem; thus the theory has recently sometimes been called "Bio-Ecological Systems Theory." Per this theoretical construction, each system contains roles, norms and rules which may shape psychological development.

Attachment	In Attachment theory psychology, Attachment is a product of the activity of a number of behavioral systems that have proximity to a person, e.g. a mother, as a predictable outcome. The concept of there being an "Attachment" behavior, stage, and process, to which a growing person remains in proximity to another was developed beginning in 1956 by British developmental psychologist John Bowlby. According to Bowlby, the concept of proximity Attachment has its origins in Charles Darwin"s 1856 Origin of Species, which "sees instinctive behavior as the outcome of behavioral structures that are activated by certain conditions and terminated by other conditions", Sigmund Freud"s 1905 Three Essays on the Theory of Sexuality and his 1915 Instincts and their Vicissitudes, which according to Bowlby "postulates part-instincts, differentiates the aim of an instinct, namely the conditions that terminate instinctive behavior, and its function, and notes how labile are the objects towards which any particular sort of instinctive behavior is directed", and Konrad Lorenz"s 1937 theory of imprinting.
Parenting	Parenting is the process of promoting and supporting the physical, emotional, social, and intellectual development of a child from infancy to adulthood. Parenting refers to the activity of raising a child rather than the biological relationship. In the case of humans, it is usually done by the biological parents of the child in question, although governments and society take a role as well.
Learning	Learning is acquiring new knowledge, behaviors, skills, values, preferences or understanding, and may involve synthesizing different types of information. The ability to learn is possessed by humans, animals and some machines. Progress over time tends to follow Learning curves.
Parent	A Parent is a mother or father; one who sires or gives birth to and/or nurtures and raises an offspring. The different roles of Parent s vary throughout the tree of life, and are especially complex in human culture. Like mothers, fathers may be categorised according to their biological, social or legal relationship with the child.
Adolescence	Adolescence is a transitional stage of physical and mental human development that occurs between childhood and adulthood. This transition involves biological (i.e. pubertal), social, and psychological changes, though the biological or physiological ones are the easiest to measure objectively. Historically, puberty has been heavily associated with teenagers and the onset of adolescent development.
Corporal punishment	Corporal punishment is the deliberate infliction of pain intended to discipline or reform a wrongdoer or change a person"s bad attitude and/or bad behaviour. The term usually refers to methodically striking the offender with an implement, whether in judicial, domestic, or educational settings. Corporal punishment may be divided into three main types: • parental or domestic Corporal punishment, i.e. the spanking of children within the family; • school Corporal punishment, i.e. of school students by teachers or other school officials; • judicial Corporal punishment, involving the official caning or whipping of convicted offenders (whether adult or juvenile) by order of a court of law.

The Corporal punishment of minors within the home is lawful in all 50 of the United States and, according to a 2000 survey, it is widely approved by parents. It has been officially outlawed in 24 countries around the world.

Peer pressure	Peer pressure refers to the influence exerted by a peer group in encouraging a person to change his or her attitudes, values, or behavior in order to conform to group norms. Social groups affected include membership groups, when the individual is "formally" a member (for example, political party, trade union), or a social clique. A person affected by Peer pressure may or may not want to belong to these groups.
Play	Play is a rite and a quality of mind in engaging with one"s worldview. Play refers to a range of voluntary, intrinsically motivated activities that are normally associated with pleasure and enjoyment. Play may consist of amusing, pretend or imaginary interpersonal and intrapersonal interactions or interplay.
High school	High school is the name used in some parts of the world (in particular the United Kingdom, Northern America and also Oceania) to describe an institution which provides all or part of secondary education. The term "High school" originated in Scotland, Great Britain with the world"s oldest being the Royal High school in 1505, and spread to the New World countries as the high prestige that the Scottish educational system had at the time led several countries to employ Scottish educators to develop their state education systems.
	The Royal High school was used as a model for the first public High school in the United States, the English High school founded in Boston, Massachusetts, in 1821.
Pregnancy	Pregnancy is the carrying of one or more offspring inside the uterus of a female. In a Pregnancy, there can be multiple gestations, as in the case of twins or triplets. Human Pregnancy is the most studied of all mammalian pregnancies.
Childhood	Childhood is a broad term usually applied to the phase of development in humans between infancy and adulthood.
	In many countries there is an age of majority when Childhood ends and a person legally becomes an adult. The age can range anywhere from 13 to 21, with 18 being the most common.
Early childhood	Early childhood is a stage in human development. It generally includes toddlerhood and some time afterwards. Play age is an unspecific designation approximately within the scope of Early childhood.
Display rules	Display rules are a social group"s informal norms about when, where, and how one should express emotions.
	Expressions of emotions vary to a great degree and hold significant meaning with great value of determining ones cultural and social identity. Display rules identify these expressions to a precise situation in a suitable context.

Child	A Child (plural: Child ren) is a human being between the stages of birth and puberty. The legal definition of Child generally refers to a minor, otherwise known as a person younger than the age of majority. Child may also describe a relationship with a parent or authority figure, or signify group membership in a clan, tribe, or religion; it can also signify being strongly affected by a specific time, place, or circumstance, as in "a Child of nature" or "a Child of the Sixties." The United Nations Convention on the Rights of the Child defines a Child as "every human being below the age of 18 years unless under the law applicable to the Child majority is attained earlier." Biologically, a Child is anyone in the developmental stage of Child hood, between infancy and adulthood.
Adult	The term Adult has at least three distinct meanings. It can indicate a biologically grown or mature person. It may also mean a plant, animal, or person who has reached full growth or alternatively is capable of reproduction, or the classification legal Adult, generally determined as a person who has attained the legally fixed age of majority; as opposed to a minor.
Puberty	Puberty refers to the process of physical changes by which a child"s body becomes an adult body capable of reproduction. Puberty is initiated by hormone signals from the brain to the gonads (the ovaries and testes.) In response, the gonads produce a variety of hormones that stimulate the growth, function, or transformation of brain, bones, muscle, skin, breasts, and reproductive organs.
Grandparents	Grandparents are the father or mother of a person"s own father or mother. Everyone has a maximum of four genetic Grandparents, eight genetic great-Grandparents, sixteen genetic great-great-Grandparents, etc. Sometimes these numbers are lower and in the case of having only two or three Grandparents sibling or half-sibling incest would be incorporated.
Sibling	A Sibling is a brother or a sister; that is, any person who shares at least one of the same parents. In most societies throughout the world, Sibling s usually grow up together and spend a good deal of their childhood with each other. This genetic and physical closeness may be marked by the development of strong emotional associations such as love or enmity.
Sibling relationships	Judy Dunn (a leading expert on sibling relationship) in 2007 described three important characteristics of Sibling relationships. Emotional quality of the relatioship: Both intensive postiive and negative emotions are often expressed by siblings toward each other. Many children and adolescents have mixed feelings toward their siblings.
Head Start	Head Start is a program of the United States Department of Health and Human Services that provides comprehensive education, health, nutrition, and parent involvement services to low-income children and their families. Head Start began in 1964 and was later updated by the Head Start Act of 1981. It is the longest-running program to address systemic poverty in the United States.

Adult	The term Adult has at least three distinct meanings. It can indicate a biologically grown or mature person. It may also mean a plant, animal, or person who has reached full growth or alternatively is capable of reproduction, or the classification legal Adult, generally determined as a person who has attained the legally fixed age of majority; as opposed to a minor.
Gender schema theory	The Gender schema theory proposes that children learn from the culture in which they live a concept of what it means to be men and women. In other words, children adjust their behavior according to their gender norms and expectations. This theory states that the developing child internalizes gender lenses that are embedded in the discourse and social practices of the culture, and that these lenses predispose the individual to construct a self-identity that is consistent with these lenses.
Learning	Learning is acquiring new knowledge, behaviors, skills, values, preferences or understanding, and may involve synthesizing different types of information. The ability to learn is possessed by humans, animals and some machines. Progress over time tends to follow Learning curves.
Play	Play is a rite and a quality of mind in engaging with one"s worldview. Play refers to a range of voluntary, intrinsically motivated activities that are normally associated with pleasure and enjoyment. Play may consist of amusing, pretend or imaginary interpersonal and intrapersonal interactions or interplay.
Childhood	Childhood is a broad term usually applied to the phase of development in humans between infancy and adulthood. In many countries there is an age of majority when Childhood ends and a person legally becomes an adult. The age can range anywhere from 13 to 21, with 18 being the most common.
Early childhood	Early childhood is a stage in human development. It generally includes toddlerhood and some time afterwards. Play age is an unspecific designation approximately within the scope of Early childhood.

Stereotypes	Throughout the history of film, television and 20th century literature, a set of stereotypes regarding the personalities of teenagers have been established, reflecting the personalities of actual teenagers in real life.

- The Dumb blonde
- The Girl next door
- The Goth girl
- The Nerd girl
- The Queen Bee
- The Surfer chick
- The Tomboy

- The Delinquent/Bad boy
- The Boy next door
- The Hunk
- The Jock
- The Stoner

- The Know-it-all
- The Party animal
- The Goth
- The Bully
- The Basket case
- The Geek
- The Wannabee
- The Overachiever
- The Nerd

.

Girl	A Girl is any female human from birth through childhood and adolescence to attainment of adulthood. The term may also be used to mean a young woman. The word Girl first appeared during the Middle Ages between 1250 and 1300 CE and came from the Anglo-Saxon words gerle , likely cognate with the Old Low German word gör (sometimes given as kerl.)
Adolescence	Adolescence is a transitional stage of physical and mental human development that occurs between childhood and adulthood. This transition involves biological (i.e. pubertal), social, and psychological changes, though the biological or physiological ones are the easiest to measure objectively. Historically, puberty has been heavily associated with teenagers and the onset of adolescent development.

Attachment	In Attachment theory psychology, Attachment is a product of the activity of a number of behavioral systems that have proximity to a person, e.g. a mother, as a predictable outcome. The concept of there being an "Attachment" behavior, stage, and process, to which a growing person remains in proximity to another was developed beginning in 1956 by British developmental psychologist John Bowlby. According to Bowlby, the concept of proximity Attachment has its origins in Charles Darwin"s 1856 Origin of Species, which "sees instinctive behavior as the outcome of behavioral structures that are activated by certain conditions and terminated by other conditions", Sigmund Freud"s 1905 Three Essays on the Theory of Sexuality and his 1915 Instincts and their Vicissitudes, which according to Bowlby "postulates part-instincts, differentiates the aim of an instinct, namely the conditions that terminate instinctive behavior, and its function, and notes how labile are the objects towards which any particular sort of instinctive behavior is directed", and Konrad Lorenz"s 1937 theory of imprinting.
Childbirth	Childbirth is the culmination of a human pregnancy or gestation period with birth of one or more newborn infants from a woman"s uterus. The process of normal human Childbirth is categorized in three stages of labour: the shortening and dilation of the cervix, descent and birth of the infant, and birth of the placenta.. In some cases, Childbirth is achieved through caesarean section, the removal of the neonate through a surgical incision in the abdomen, rather than through vaginal birth.
Child	A Child (plural: Child ren) is a human being between the stages of birth and puberty. The legal definition of Child generally refers to a minor, otherwise known as a person younger than the age of majority. Child may also describe a relationship with a parent or authority figure, or signify group membership in a clan, tribe, or religion; it can also signify being strongly affected by a specific time, place, or circumstance, as in "a Child of nature" or "a Child of the Sixties." The United Nations Convention on the Rights of the Child defines a Child as "every human being below the age of 18 years unless under the law applicable to the Child majority is attained earlier." Biologically, a Child is anyone in the developmental stage of Child hood, between infancy and adulthood.
Parent	A Parent is a mother or father; one who sires or gives birth to and/or nurtures and raises an offspring. The different roles of Parent s vary throughout the tree of life, and are especially complex in human culture. Like mothers, fathers may be categorised according to their biological, social or legal relationship with the child.
Mother	A Mother is a biological and/or social female parent of an offspring. Because of the complexity and differences of the social, cultural, and religious definitions and roles, it is challenging to define a Mother in a universally accepted definition. In the case of a mammal such as a human, the biological Mother gestates a fertilized ovum, which is called first an embryo, and then a fetus.
Family planning	Family planning is the planning of when to have children, and the use of birth control and other techniques to implement such plans. Other techniques commonly used include sexuality education, prevention and management of sexually transmitted infections, pre-conception counseling and management, and infertility management.

	Family planning is sometimes used as a synonym for the use of birth control, though it often includes more.
Sibling	A Sibling is a brother or a sister; that is, any person who shares at least one of the same parents. In most societies throughout the world, Sibling s usually grow up together and spend a good deal of their childhood with each other. This genetic and physical closeness may be marked by the development of strong emotional associations such as love or enmity.
Sibling relationships	Judy Dunn (a leading expert on sibling relationship) in 2007 described three important characteristics of Sibling relationships. Emotional quality of the relatioship: Both intensive postiive and negative emotions are often expressed by siblings toward each other. Many children and adolescents have mixed feelings toward their siblings.
Extended Family	Extended family is a term with several distinct meanings. First, it is used synonymously with consanguineous family. Second, in societies dominated by the conjugal family, it is used to refer to kindred who does not belong to the conjugal family.
Conservation	Conservation refers to an ability in logical thinking according to the psychologist Jean Piaget who developed four stages in cognitive development. During third stage, the Concrete operational stage, the child of age 7-11 masters this ability, to logically determine that a certain quantity will remain the same despite adjustment of the container, shape, or apparent size. Conservation earned its name thanks to Jean Piaget, the psychologist responsible for the stages of development.
Autism	Autism is a brain development disorder characterized by impaired social interaction and communication, and by restricted and repetitive behavior. These signs all begin before a child is three years old. Autism affects many parts of the brain; how this occurs is not understood.
Intelligence	Intelligence is an umbrella term used to describe a property of the mind that encompasses many related abilities, such as the capacities to reason, to plan, to solve problems, to think abstractly, to comprehend ideas, to use language, and to learn. There are several ways to define Intelligence. In some cases, Intelligence may include traits such as creativity, personality, character, knowledge, or wisdom.
Puberty	Puberty refers to the process of physical changes by which a child"s body becomes an adult body capable of reproduction. Puberty is initiated by hormone signals from the brain to the gonads (the ovaries and testes.) In response, the gonads produce a variety of hormones that stimulate the growth, function, or transformation of brain, bones, muscle, skin, breasts, and reproductive organs.

Grandparents	Grandparents are the father or mother of a person"s own father or mother. Everyone has a maximum of four genetic Grandparents, eight genetic great-Grandparents, sixteen genetic great-great-Grandparents, etc. Sometimes these numbers are lower and in the case of having only two or three Grandparents sibling or half-sibling incest would be incorporated.
Parent	A Parent is a mother or father; one who sires or gives birth to and/or nurtures and raises an offspring. The different roles of Parent s vary throughout the tree of life, and are especially complex in human culture. Like mothers, fathers may be categorised according to their biological, social or legal relationship with the child.
Sibling	A Sibling is a brother or a sister; that is, any person who shares at least one of the same parents. In most societies throughout the world, Sibling s usually grow up together and spend a good deal of their childhood with each other. This genetic and physical closeness may be marked by the development of strong emotional associations such as love or enmity.
Sibling relationships	Judy Dunn (a leading expert on sibling relationship) in 2007 described three important characteristics of Sibling relationships. Emotional quality of the relatioship: Both intensive postiive and negative emotions are often expressed by siblings toward each other. Many children and adolescents have mixed feelings toward their siblings.
Child	A Child (plural: Child ren) is a human being between the stages of birth and puberty. The legal definition of Child generally refers to a minor, otherwise known as a person younger than the age of majority. Child may also describe a relationship with a parent or authority figure, or signify group membership in a clan, tribe, or religion; it can also signify being strongly affected by a specific time, place, or circumstance, as in "a Child of nature" or "a Child of the Sixties." The United Nations Convention on the Rights of the Child defines a Child as "every human being below the age of 18 years unless under the law applicable to the Child majority is attained earlier." Biologically, a Child is anyone in the developmental stage of Child hood, between infancy and adulthood.
Ecological systems theory	Ecological Systems Theory specifies four types of nested environmental systems, with bi-directional influences within and between the systems. The theory was developed by Urie Bronfenbrenner, generally regarded as one of the world"s leading scholars in the field of developmental psychology. The four systems: • Microsystem: Immediate environments • Mesosystem: A system comprising connections between immediate environments • Exosystem: External environmental settings which only indirectly affect development • Macrosystem: The larger cultural context

Later, a fifth system was added:

- Chronosystem: The patterning of environmental events and transitions over the course of life. The person"s own biology may be considered part of the microsystem; thus the theory has recently sometimes been called "Bio-Ecological Systems Theory."

Per this theoretical construction, each system contains roles, norms and rules which may shape psychological development.

Adolescence	Adolescence is a transitional stage of physical and mental human development that occurs between childhood and adulthood. This transition involves biological (i.e. pubertal), social, and psychological changes, though the biological or physiological ones are the easiest to measure objectively. Historically, puberty has been heavily associated with teenagers and the onset of adolescent development.
Attachment	In Attachment theory psychology, Attachment is a product of the activity of a number of behavioral systems that have proximity to a person, e.g. a mother, as a predictable outcome. The concept of there being an "Attachment" behavior, stage, and process, to which a growing person remains in proximity to another was developed beginning in 1956 by British developmental psychologist John Bowlby. According to Bowlby, the concept of proximity Attachment has its origins in Charles Darwin"s 1856 Origin of Species, which "sees instinctive behavior as the outcome of behavioral structures that are activated by certain conditions and terminated by other conditions", Sigmund Freud"s 1905 Three Essays on the Theory of Sexuality and his 1915 Instincts and their Vicissitudes, which according to Bowlby "postulates part-instincts, differentiates the aim of an instinct, namely the conditions that terminate instinctive behavior, and its function, and notes how labile are the objects towards which any particular sort of instinctive behavior is directed", and Konrad Lorenz"s 1937 theory of imprinting.
Father	A Father is defined as a male parent of an offspring. The adjective "paternal" refers to Father parallel to "maternal" for mother. The Father child relationship is the defining factor of the Father hood role.
Mother	A Mother is a biological and/or social female parent of an offspring. Because of the complexity and differences of the social, cultural, and religious definitions and roles, it is challenging to define a Mother in a universally accepted definition. In the case of a mammal such as a human, the biological Mother gestates a fertilized ovum, which is called first an embryo, and then a fetus.
Puberty	Puberty refers to the process of physical changes by which a child"s body becomes an adult body capable of reproduction. Puberty is initiated by hormone signals from the brain to the gonads (the ovaries and testes.) In response, the gonads produce a variety of hormones that stimulate the growth, function, or transformation of brain, bones, muscle, skin, breasts, and reproductive organs.

Parental leave	Parental leave is an employee benefit that provides paid or unpaid time off work to care for a child or make arrangements for the child"s welfare. Often, the term Parental leave includes maternity, paternity, and adoption leave. In most western countries Parental leave is available for those who have worked for their current employer for a certain period of time.
Infant	An Infant or baby is the term used to refer to the very young offspring of humans and other primates. The term Infant derives from the Latin word infans, meaning "unable to speak." It is typically applied to children between the ages of 1 month and 12 months . However, definitions vary between birth and 3 years of age.
Parenting	Parenting is the process of promoting and supporting the physical, emotional, social, and intellectual development of a child from infancy to adulthood. Parenting refers to the activity of raising a child rather than the biological relationship. In the case of humans, it is usually done by the biological parents of the child in question, although governments and society take a role as well.
Childbirth	Childbirth is the culmination of a human pregnancy or gestation period with birth of one or more newborn infants from a woman"s uterus. The process of normal human Childbirth is categorized in three stages of labour: the shortening and dilation of the cervix, descent and birth of the infant, and birth of the placenta.. In some cases, Childbirth is achieved through caesarean section, the removal of the neonate through a surgical incision in the abdomen, rather than through vaginal birth.
Early childhood	Early childhood is a stage in human development. It generally includes toddlerhood and some time afterwards. Play age is an unspecific designation approximately within the scope of Early childhood.
Intelligence	Intelligence is an umbrella term used to describe a property of the mind that encompasses many related abilities, such as the capacities to reason, to plan, to solve problems, to think abstractly, to comprehend ideas, to use language, and to learn. There are several ways to define Intelligence. In some cases, Intelligence may include traits such as creativity, personality, character, knowledge, or wisdom.
Play	Play is a rite and a quality of mind in engaging with one"s worldview. Play refers to a range of voluntary, intrinsically motivated activities that are normally associated with pleasure and enjoyment. Play may consist of amusing, pretend or imaginary interpersonal and intrapersonal interactions or interplay.
Youth	Youth is the period between childhood and adulthood, described as the period of physical and psychological development from the onset of puberty to maturity and early adulthood. Definitions of the specific age range that constitutes Youth vary. An individual"s actual maturity may not correspond to their chronological age, as immature individuals exist at all ages.

Nuclear family	The term Nuclear family is used to distinguish a family group consisting of most commonly, a father and mother and their children, from what is known as an extended family. Nuclear families can be any size, as long as the family can support itself and there are only children and two parents, nuclear families meet its individual members" basic needs since available resources are only divided among few individuals or the family would be known as an extended family. Nuclear Families are uncommon in the Middle East.
Family planning	Family planning is the planning of when to have children, and the use of birth control and other techniques to implement such plans. Other techniques commonly used include sexuality education, prevention and management of sexually transmitted infections, pre-conception counseling and management, and infertility management. Family planning is sometimes used as a synonym for the use of birth control, though it often includes more.
Extended family	Extended family is a term with several distinct meanings. First, it is used synonymously with consanguineous family. Second, in societies dominated by the conjugal family, it is used to refer to kindred who does not belong to the conjugal family.
Sibling rivalry	Sibling rivalry is a type of competition or animosity among brothers and sisters, blood-related or not. 82% of people in Western countries have at least one sibling, and siblings generally spend more time together during childhood than they do with parents. The sibling bond is often complicated and is influenced by factors such as parental treatment, birth order, personality, and people and experiences outside the family.
Child support	In family law and government policy, Child support or child maintenance is the ongoing obligation for a periodic payment made directly or indirectly by an ("obligor") to an ("obligee") for the financial care and support of children of a relationship or marriage that has been terminated, or in some cases never existed. Oftentimes, but not always, the obligor is a non-custodial parent. Oftentimes, but not always, the obligee is a custodial parent, caregiver or guardian, or the government.
Child custody	Child custody and guardianship are legal terms which are sometimes used to describe the legal and practical relationship between a parent and his or her child, such as the right of the parent to make decisions for the child, and the parent"s duty to care for the child. Following ratification of the United Nations Convention on the Rights of the Child in most countries, terms such as "residence" and "contact" (known as "visitation" in the United States) have superseded the concepts of "custody" and "access". Instead of a parent having "custody" of or "access" to a child, a child is now said to "reside" or have "contact" with a parent.

Stereotypes	Throughout the history of film, television and 20th century literature, a set of stereotypes regarding the personalities of teenagers have been established, reflecting the personalities of actual teenagers in real life.

- The Dumb blonde
- The Girl next door
- The Goth girl
- The Nerd girl
- The Queen Bee
- The Surfer chick
- The Tomboy

- The Delinquent/Bad boy
- The Boy next door
- The Hunk
- The Jock
- The Stoner

- The Know-it-all
- The Party animal
- The Goth
- The Bully
- The Basket case
- The Geek
- The Wannabee
- The Overachiever
- The Nerd

Marriage	Marriage is a social union of individuals that creates kinship. This union may also be called matrimony, while the ceremony that marks its beginning is usually called a wedding and the married status created is sometimes called wedlock. Marriage is an institution in which interpersonal relationships (usually intimate and sexual) are acknowledged by a variety of ways, depending on the culture or demographic.
Head Start	Head Start is a program of the United States Department of Health and Human Services that provides comprehensive education, health, nutrition, and parent involvement services to low-income children and their families. Head Start began in 1964 and was later updated by the Head Start Act of 1981. It is the longest-running program to address systemic poverty in the United States.

Developmental disability	Developmental disability is a term used to describe life-long, disabilities attributable to mental and/or physical or combination of mental and physical impairments, manifested prior to age 18. The term is used most commonly in the United States to refer to disabilities affecting daily functioning in three or more of the following areas:

- capacity for independent living
- economic self-sufficiency
- learning
- mobility
- receptive and expressive language
- self-care
- self-direction

The term first appeared in U.S. law in 1970, when Congress used the term to describe the population of individuals who had historically been placed in state institutions, in its effort to improve conditions in these dehumanizing facilities (P.L. 91-517, "The Developmental Disabilities Services and Facilities Construction Act of 1970".) The law has since been amended many times, and now calls for the full community inclusion and self-determination of people with developmental disabilities (P.L. 106-402.) Frequently, people with mental retardation, cerebral palsy, autism spectrum disorder, various genetic and chromosomal disorders such as Down syndrome and Fragile X syndrome, and Fetal Alcohol Spectrum Disorder are described as having developmental disabilities.

Attention-deficit/hyperactivity disorder	Attention-deficit/hyperactivity disorder is a neurobehavioral developmental disorder. Attention-deficit/hyperactivity disorderHD is defined as a "persistent pattern of inattention or hyperactivity--impulsivity that is more frequently displayed and more severe than is typically observed in individuals at a comparable level of development." While symptoms may appear innocent and merely annoying nuisances to observers, "if left untreated, the persistent and pervasive effects of Attention-deficit/hyperactivity disorderHD symptoms can insidiously and severely interfere with one"s ability to get the most out of education, fulfill one"s potential in the workplace, establish and maintain interpersonal relationships, and maintain a generally positive sense of self."[:p.2] It is the most commonly diagnosed behavioral disorder in children, affecting about 3 to 5% of children globally with symptoms starting before seven years of age. Attention-deficit/hyperactivity disorderHD is generally a chronic disorder with 30 to 50% of those individuals diagnosed in childhood continuing to have symptoms into adulthood.
Autism	Autism is a brain development disorder characterized by impaired social interaction and communication, and by restricted and repetitive behavior. These signs all begin before a child is three years old. Autism affects many parts of the brain; how this occurs is not understood.
Corporal punishment	Corporal punishment is the deliberate infliction of pain intended to discipline or reform a wrongdoer or change a person"s bad attitude and/or bad behaviour. The term usually refers to methodically striking the offender with an implement, whether in judicial, domestic, or educational settings.

Corporal punishment may be divided into three main types:

- parental or domestic Corporal punishment, i.e. the spanking of children within the family;
- school Corporal punishment, i.e. of school students by teachers or other school officials;
- judicial Corporal punishment, involving the official caning or whipping of convicted offenders (whether adult or juvenile) by order of a court of law.

The Corporal punishment of minors within the home is lawful in all 50 of the United States and, according to a 2000 survey, it is widely approved by parents. It has been officially outlawed in 24 countries around the world.

Day care

Day care or child care is care of a child during the day by a person other than the child"s legal guardians, typically performed by someone outside the child"s immediate family. Day care is typically an ongoing service during specific periods, such as the parents" time at work.

The service is known as child care in the United Kingdom and Australia and Day care in North America (although child care also has a broader meaning.)

Play	Play is a rite and a quality of mind in engaging with one"s worldview. Play refers to a range of voluntary, intrinsically motivated activities that are normally associated with pleasure and enjoyment. Play may consist of amusing, pretend or imaginary interpersonal and intrapersonal interactions or interplay.
Attachment	In Attachment theory psychology, Attachment is a product of the activity of a number of behavioral systems that have proximity to a person, e.g. a mother, as a predictable outcome. The concept of there being an "Attachment" behavior, stage, and process, to which a growing person remains in proximity to another was developed beginning in 1956 by British developmental psychologist John Bowlby. According to Bowlby, the concept of proximity Attachment has its origins in Charles Darwin"s 1856 Origin of Species, which "sees instinctive behavior as the outcome of behavioral structures that are activated by certain conditions and terminated by other conditions", Sigmund Freud"s 1905 Three Essays on the Theory of Sexuality and his 1915 Instincts and their Vicissitudes, which according to Bowlby "postulates part-instincts, differentiates the aim of an instinct, namely the conditions that terminate instinctive behavior, and its function, and notes how labile are the objects towards which any particular sort of instinctive behavior is directed", and Konrad Lorenz"s 1937 theory of imprinting.
Childhood	Childhood is a broad term usually applied to the phase of development in humans between infancy and adulthood. In many countries there is an age of majority when Childhood ends and a person legally becomes an adult. The age can range anywhere from 13 to 21, with 18 being the most common.
Early childhood	Early childhood is a stage in human development. It generally includes toddlerhood and some time afterwards. Play age is an unspecific designation approximately within the scope of Early childhood.
Parallel play	Parallel play is a concept from developmental psychology. It means children playing side by side without interaction. It is commonly seen among children of ages 2 or 3.
Autism	Autism is a brain development disorder characterized by impaired social interaction and communication, and by restricted and repetitive behavior. These signs all begin before a child is three years old. Autism affects many parts of the brain; how this occurs is not understood.
Intelligence	Intelligence is an umbrella term used to describe a property of the mind that encompasses many related abilities, such as the capacities to reason, to plan, to solve problems, to think abstractly, to comprehend ideas, to use language, and to learn. There are several ways to define Intelligence. In some cases, Intelligence may include traits such as creativity, personality, character, knowledge, or wisdom.
Adolescence	Adolescence is a transitional stage of physical and mental human development that occurs between childhood and adulthood. This transition involves biological (i.e. pubertal), social, and psychological changes, though the biological or physiological ones are the easiest to measure objectively. Historically, puberty has been heavily associated with teenagers and the onset of adolescent development.

Adult	The term Adult has at least three distinct meanings. It can indicate a biologically grown or mature person. It may also mean a plant, animal, or person who has reached full growth or alternatively is capable of reproduction, or the classification legal Adult, generally determined as a person who has attained the legally fixed age of majority; as opposed to a minor.
Theory of cognitive development	The Theory of cognitive development, first developed by Jean Piaget, proposes that there are four distinct, increasingly sophisticated stages of mental representation that children pass through on their way to an adult level of intelligence.
	The four stages, roughly correlated with age, are as follows:
	<ul><li>Sensorimotor period (years 0 to 2)</li><li>Preoperational period (years 2 to 7)</li><li>Concrete operational period (years 7 to 12)</li><li>Formal operational period (years 12 and up)</li></ul>
	The Sensorimotor Stage is the first of the four stages of cognitive development. "In this stage, infants construct an understanding of the world by coordinating sensory experiences with physical, motoric actions." "Infants gain knowledge of the world from the physical actions they perform on it." "An infant progresses from reflexive, instinctual action at birth to the beginning of symbolic thought toward the end of the stage." "Piaget divided the sensorimotor stage into six sub-stages":
	"By the end of the sensorimotor period, objects are both separate from the self and permanent." "Object permanence is the understanding that objects continue to exist even when they cannot be seen, heard, or touched." "Acquiring the sense of object permanence is one of the infant"s most important accomplishments, according to Piaget."
	The Preoperational stage is the second of four stages of cognitive development. By observing sequences of play, Piaget was able to demonstrate that towards the end of the second year, a qualitatively new kind of psychological functioning occurs.
Child	A Child (plural: Child ren) is a human being between the stages of birth and puberty. The legal definition of Child generally refers to a minor, otherwise known as a person younger than the age of majority. Child may also describe a relationship with a parent or authority figure, or signify group membership in a clan, tribe, or religion; it can also signify being strongly affected by a specific time, place, or circumstance, as in "a Child of nature" or "a Child of the Sixties."
	The United Nations Convention on the Rights of the Child defines a Child as "every human being below the age of 18 years unless under the law applicable to the Child majority is attained earlier." Biologically, a Child is anyone in the developmental stage of Child hood, between infancy and adulthood.
Display rules	Display rules are a social group"s informal norms about when, where, and how one should express emotions.
	Expressions of emotions vary to a great degree and hold significant meaning with great value of determining ones cultural and social identity. Display rules identify these expressions to a precise situation in a suitable context.

Parent	A Parent is a mother or father; one who sires or gives birth to and/or nurtures and raises an offspring. The different roles of Parent s vary throughout the tree of life, and are especially complex in human culture.
	Like mothers, fathers may be categorised according to their biological, social or legal relationship with the child.
Emerging adulthood	Emerging adulthood is a phase of the life span between adolescence and full-fledged adulthood, proposed by Jeffrey Arnett in a 2000 article in the American Psychologist (summary of article 469.)
Attention-deficit/hyperactivity disorder	Attention-deficit/hyperactivity disorder is a neurobehavioral developmental disorder. Attention-deficit/hyperactivity disorderHD is defined as a "persistent pattern of inattention or hyperactivity--impulsivity that is more frequently displayed and more severe than is typically observed in individuals at a comparable level of development." While symptoms may appear innocent and merely annoying nuisances to observers, "if left untreated, the persistent and pervasive effects of Attention-deficit/hyperactivity disorderHD symptoms can insidiously and severely interfere with one"s ability to get the most out of education, fulfill one"s potential in the workplace, establish and maintain interpersonal relationships, and maintain a generally positive sense of self."[p.2]
	It is the most commonly diagnosed behavioral disorder in children, affecting about 3 to 5% of children globally with symptoms starting before seven years of age. Attention-deficit/hyperactivity disorderHD is generally a chronic disorder with 30 to 50% of those individuals diagnosed in childhood continuing to have symptoms into adulthood.
Mother	A Mother is a biological and/or social female parent of an offspring. Because of the complexity and differences of the social, cultural, and religious definitions and roles, it is challenging to define a Mother in a universally accepted definition.
	In the case of a mammal such as a human, the biological Mother gestates a fertilized ovum, which is called first an embryo, and then a fetus.
Clique	A Clique is an exclusive group of people who share interests, views, purposes, patterns of behavior, or ethnicity. A Clique as a reference group can be either normative or comparative. Membership in a Clique is often, but not necessarily, exclusive, and qualifications for membership may be social or essential to the nature of the Clique.
Peer pressure	Peer pressure refers to the influence exerted by a peer group in encouraging a person to change his or her attitudes, values, or behavior in order to conform to group norms. Social groups affected include membership groups, when the individual is "formally" a member (for example, political party, trade union), or a social clique. A person affected by Peer pressure may or may not want to belong to these groups.
Parenting	Parenting is the process of promoting and supporting the physical, emotional, social, and intellectual development of a child from infancy to adulthood. Parenting refers to the activity of raising a child rather than the biological relationship.

	In the case of humans, it is usually done by the biological parents of the child in question, although governments and society take a role as well.
Grandparents	Grandparents are the father or mother of a person"s own father or mother. Everyone has a maximum of four genetic Grandparents, eight genetic great-Grandparents, sixteen genetic great-great-Grandparents, etc. Sometimes these numbers are lower and in the case of having only two or three Grandparents sibling or half-sibling incest would be incorporated.
Head Start	Head Start is a program of the United States Department of Health and Human Services that provides comprehensive education, health, nutrition, and parent involvement services to low-income children and their families. Head Start began in 1964 and was later updated by the Head Start Act of 1981. It is the longest-running program to address systemic poverty in the United States.
Puberty	Puberty refers to the process of physical changes by which a child"s body becomes an adult body capable of reproduction. Puberty is initiated by hormone signals from the brain to the gonads (the ovaries and testes.) In response, the gonads produce a variety of hormones that stimulate the growth, function, or transformation of brain, bones, muscle, skin, breasts, and reproductive organs.
Sibling	A Sibling is a brother or a sister; that is, any person who shares at least one of the same parents. In most societies throughout the world, Sibling s usually grow up together and spend a good deal of their childhood with each other. This genetic and physical closeness may be marked by the development of strong emotional associations such as love or enmity.
Sibling relationships	Judy Dunn (a leading expert on sibling relationship) in 2007 described three important characteristics of Sibling relationships. Emotional quality of the relatioship: Both intensive postiive and negative emotions are often expressed by siblings toward each other. Many children and adolescents have mixed feelings toward their siblings.
Pregnancy	Pregnancy is the carrying of one or more offspring inside the uterus of a female. In a Pregnancy, there can be multiple gestations, as in the case of twins or triplets. Human Pregnancy is the most studied of all mammalian pregnancies.
Teenage pregnancy	Teenage pregnancy is defined as a teenaged or underage girl (usually within the ages of 13-19) becoming pregnant. The term in everyday speech usually refers to women who have not reached legal adulthood, which varies across the world, who become pregnant. The average age of menarche (first menstrual period) in the United States is 12 years old, though this figure varies by ethnicity and weight, and first ovulation occurs only irregularly until after this.
Youth	Youth is the period between childhood and adulthood, described as the period of physical and psychological development from the onset of puberty to maturity and early adulthood. Definitions of the specific age range that constitutes Youth vary. An individual"s actual maturity may not correspond to their chronological age, as immature individuals exist at all ages.

Learning	Learning is acquiring new knowledge, behaviors, skills, values, preferences or understanding, and may involve synthesizing different types of information. The ability to learn is possessed by humans, animals and some machines. Progress over time tends to follow Learning curves.
V-Chip	V-chip is a generic term used for television receivers allowing the blocking of programs based on their ratings category. It is intended for use by parents to manage their children"s television viewing. Most 13-inch and larger televisions manufactured for the United States market since 1999 and all units as of January 2000 are required to have the V-chip technology.
High School	High school is the name used in some parts of the world (in particular the United Kingdom, Northern America and also Oceania) to describe an institution which provides all or part of secondary education. The term "High school" originated in Scotland, Great Britain with the world"s oldest being the Royal High school in 1505, and spread to the New World countries as the high prestige that the Scottish educational system had at the time led several countries to employ Scottish educators to develop their state education systems. The Royal High school was used as a model for the first public High school in the United States, the English High school founded in Boston, Massachusetts, in 1821.
Kindergarten	In each state of Australia, Kindergarten means something slightly different. In New South Wales and the Australian Capital Territory, it is the first year of primary school. In Victoria, Kindergarten is a form of preschool and may be referred to interchangeably as preschool or Kindergarten.
Childbirth	Childbirth is the culmination of a human pregnancy or gestation period with birth of one or more newborn infants from a woman"s uterus. The process of normal human Childbirth is categorized in three stages of labour: the shortening and dilation of the cervix, descent and birth of the infant, and birth of the placenta.. In some cases, Childbirth is achieved through caesarean section, the removal of the neonate through a surgical incision in the abdomen, rather than through vaginal birth.
Mental retardation	Mental retardation is a generalized disorder, characterized by subaverage cognitive functioning and deficits in two or more adaptive behaviors with onset before the age of 18. Once focused almost entirely on cognition, the definition now includes both a component relating to mental functioning and one relating to individuals" functional skills in their environment. The term "Mental retardation" is a diagnostic term designed to capture and standardize a group of disconnected categories of mental functioning such as "idiot", "imbecile", and "moron" derived from early IQ tests, which acquired pejorative connotations in popular discourse over time.
Father	A Father is defined as a male parent of an offspring. The adjective "paternal" refers to Father parallel to "maternal" for mother. The Father child relationship is the defining factor of the Father hood role.

LaVergne, TN USA
23 September 2010
198008LV00002B/190/P